Help *for* Hard Times

Also by Jim Harbaugh, S.J.

A 12-Step Approach
to the Spiritual Exercises
of St. Ignatius

A 12-Step Approach
to the Sunday Readings

Help *for* Hard Times

*A Twelve-Step Path Through the
Pandemic and Random Disasters*

Jim Harbaugh, S.J.

ISBN: 978-1-7379036-0-4

To the hundreds of people on Zoom who have kept up my spirits even on days when the sun was invisible in the Bay Area.

We all got through this together.

Contents

ᕤᕥ

Foreword

This book may just change your life. If this is not something you are available for – a bigger, kinder, life, grounded in connection, dignity, authenticity – beware! If the last four or five years of Trump and rising tides and pandemic worked out for you, don't bother.

For the rest of us, this book offers a path of sanity, grace, and hope. It is sometimes playful, sometimes profound, like its author. Could the world be scarier these days, these dark and surreal days? Pandemonium and despots at the highest levels, a global plague, children in cages, cities and hearts in lockdown? Ah, I fondly remember the good old days, when we were collectively panicked about Australia in flames and polar bears floating away in the sea.

It feels like a fever dream some days, or a funhouse mirror that is about as fun as the grave. The natural response is to deny, control, obsess, isolate, those tried and true default landing zones. Without a lot of help, these seem to be the malignant comfort zones of a scared childhood, brought into maturity (a much nicer word for old age). Without help, I use them to self-medicate, like addicts use pills. For example, we may know that help is the sunny side of control, but what is usually our first response? Help, fix, rescue. We may know that peace of mind is an inside job, yet where do we so often turn? To toxic obsession with other people's behavior.

How on earth, with such troubled minds, in the face of these catastrophic changes, do we avoid shutting down, turning to our addictive substances and patterns? How do we stay faithful and present, even sometimes joyous? How do we keep our spirits from flagging, or even keeling over? How do we open our hearts to love and the glorious mysteries of life? How do we stay true to our moral callings when we are exhausted and just want to go back to bed with the kitty and donuts (not that these are a bad thing – just perhaps not every few hours).

How do we get a grip? How do we not lose faith? How do we keep going?

It helps to have a secret weapon against existential dread, and one of mine is the author of this book. Thank God Jim Harbaugh, S.J., has confronted these questions over the last couple of years, from the perspective of 12 Step Recovery, his fifty years as a Bible scholar and Jesuit, from his deep, gentle humanity, from his failures and recoveries, from mentors and cats.

He is a man of many paradoxes, brilliant and also innocent, cheerfully game and yet prone to depression, furious about injustice and very kind. He can be a lively companion, and he can be as woofily as Eeyore. He is a bit timid, yet has bravely done the deep dive into knowing his own heart, over and over again. He knows loneliness, and grace. He gives freely, and, even harder, receives.

He is very funny, and deeply serious about his calling, to know God and help God's children.

To me, he has always seemed like a man from another era, a priest who makes house calls in a worn hat, holding a Bible, walking slowly, stopping to find the source of the birdsong in the branches. I tend to be more like Snaggletooth on stage, playing Shakespeare, clutching my heart. We were made for each other.

You'll find in these pages a careful observer of the world, who searches for truth, researches all realms of history, Biblical and otherwise. And you will find someone who listens.

He listens to the people to whom he ministers. He listens to his brothers and sisters in each parish and room of recovery. He listens to each person who comes to him in pain or fear, loneliness, stuckness, and sometimes he counsels, if asked. He does not turn anyone away; rather he welcomes these moments of trust, one heart speaking to another, no matter how screwed up and crabby those hearts may be.

I should know. I am privileged to be one of those hearts.

I urged him a while ago to write a book for all of us, to offer some hope during the Trump era, direct us toward wellness in the face of our powerlessness over the madness and barbarity. I asked for a book of healing actions and attitudes as we face the pandemic, the ongoing devastation of social and economic polarization, centuries of racial oppression.

"Oh, is that all?" he asked.

This is that book, a handbook for these very hard times. It is filled with hard-fought truth, because Jim is a truth-teller. It is modest, never show-offy, although Jim has a dazzling, encyclopedic mind. And this guy can really make me laugh, even as we have cried together. Much of this book is his take on the 12 Steps, beginning with the reassurance that this is a "We" program, based in surrender and trust, in the sorrows and pleasure of the precious community, rather than our unfortunate history of rugged individualism. I've heard it said that the whole system works because we're not all nuts on the same day, and this is a book for when you are the one who feels defeated, and when you're the one hoping to offer another person's spiritual help, a little encouragement and uplift, a bit of bread for the journey.

Anne Lamott
Fairfax, California

❧❧

Why I'm Writing

I'm writing early in the Covid-19 pandemic. I live in the next county over from the first place in the United States where the virus surfaced, in a nursing home.

By a few days ago 27 of the 35 deaths from the virus in Washington State had taken place at that nursing home. Because of this, many of the restrictive responses to the pandemic began in my area. Those include closed schools, closed restaurants, and working from home. I am 74, so I am one of those who are supposed to stay at home. I have mostly done so, if only because seven of the twelve members of my Jesuit community are even older than me. But when I have occasion to go out, it's eerie to see traffic and forms of business taking place just as they did on an ordinary day two weeks ago.

Earlier today I went to the drugstore where I get my prescriptions and my annual flu shots. I got the shingles vaccine today; but the place looked no different than it did last October when I got my flu shot – same pharmacists behind the counter, same people working the checkout, same customers, mostly older since it was mid-morning. Amid so much that was the same, the thought kept circling in my head, "We are never getting back to the way things were just a little while ago. Great and irreversible changes are taking place."

As an older person largely confined to home, I have a lot of free time now. I would much rather be doing my job as a Catholic priest, but even visiting the sick – one of the few ministries still taking place person-to-person – is restricted to three of the youngest and healthiest priests locally. I simply don't qualify for that.

My last book was about spirituality and healthy aging. Now I face the diminished tasks available to an old man in a time of world crisis. So what can I do but write, the most solitary of exercises, but one that can help a lot of people nevertheless?

What I am writing was commissioned a while ago by my friend Annie Lamott. I got to know her through our mutual friend Tom Weston, S.J. The three of us share a spiritual practice of 12 Step recovery. Four years ago the three of us were on a cruise together, out of Rome to Greece and Turkey. Annie and I got to talking about the Bible. She worships with a Presbyterian community in Marin County, California; I am a Jesuit priest, like Tom. Our religious traditions come at the Bible from different angles. My tradition, which is shared by Catholics, Episcopalians, Lutherans, and a lot of other non-evangelical Christian bodies, studies the Bible in the light of the history of its composition, the nuances of the words that make it up, and the social and historical context within which it came to be.

As it happens, I once got a doctorate in the Victorian novel, so I know something about words and history.

I've had a great deal of pleasure sharing what I know about the Bible, as text and as historical product, with Annie. She is of course a very apt and funny pupil. At one point she told me that I ought to use my knowledge, both of the Bible and of 12 Step recovery, to write a book for our painful times. Mind you, this was long before anyone had heard of the coronavirus; Annie was responding to the fear and anger that has so bitterly divided the United States, and much of the rest of the world, over the last few years.

No mean feat, Annie: I just need to write a book that will comfort people and heal divisions, now that a pandemic has made the huge conflicts of a few months ago seem trivial. I am corresponding, by phone and email, with many recovering friends: a long-time mentor, Mary C., has agreed with me that when we're too scared to sleep each night at 3 a.m., we will send comforting thoughts to one another as each of us pets our cats.

And under these circumstances I'm supposed to find words to heal the world?

But because of the virus I don't have anything else much to do.

So here goes. Let's begin with what I am most afraid of now.

Chapter 1

❧

What's so Funny?

I don't think I'm afraid of dying, although one of my spiritual defects is a lack of imagination, so I may simply have failed to grasp what dying is.

But I haven't always been this fearless. As a young man, I experienced anxiety a lot, and it would take decades before that got correctly labeled as a symptom of depression. My great fear back then was of going insane.

Like many anxious seminarians and nuns at that time, I was prescribed tranquilizers – after all, this was the late 1960s, the *Mad Men* on Valium era. In the '70s I substituted alcohol for the tranquilizers, since I didn't need a prescription for that.

The result was that, by the time I was in my late thirties, I had *two* paralyzing fears: I now also feared that the drinking I did to keep insanity at bay was making me an alcoholic, like my father. I was especially mortified at that because I had gone to such great trouble to escape alcoholism, which ran in my family like the track team runs in *Juno*. For instance, I had become a Jesuit, a member of a well-respected bunch of men (including a lot of drunks, some of whom are now my closest friends, but I didn't know that until later). I also got a doctorate – from the University of Chicago, no less, one of the more ferociously snobby schools in our country – to further distance myself from my sordid genes. But instead of shielding me from alcoholism, the terror of being in that doctoral program only led me across the no-turning-back bridge to addiction (see *Zen and the Art of Motorcycle Maintenance* for a harrowing account of mental illness at the U. of C.)

FEARLESS RECOVERY

Once I realized that my worst fears had been realized, that I had in fact become alcoholic, I asked, at thirty-seven, to go to treatment. And I did – the twenty-eight-day Minnesota Model inpatient rehab that insurance covered back then.

Since I did not think it – or anything not involving ingesting substances – would really help, I made no long-range plans. I couldn't imagine life after treatment, just like I can't imagine life after the pandemic just now. They kept me an additional week in treatment precisely because I seemed fresh out of plans for life after it.

Perhaps they suspected that I actually had a plan that I wasn't sharing with them. My plan was to go home, hang out, and wait for my first anxiety attack. After that I guessed I would come back to the rehab unit and tell them that 12 Step recovery didn't work for me, so let's talk drugs.

I never came back and told them their plan for me had failed; if I had I suppose I'd still be in treatment. Instead I did what they said and began attending meetings. Oh, I had an anxiety attack or two. I'm pretty scared right now, in fact, as I mentioned before, scared like a lot of people around the world. But something changed in my relationship to my fear. It turned out that it made a huge difference to know I was not alone in my fears or in the reasons for my fears. To my surprise, their plan worked, and I haven't drunk alcohol in a very long time. In sum: My great fears led to alcoholism, which led to recovery, which led to a life that I have long suspected to be a simulation, since it seems too good to be true. I never did, nor could I have, imagined a life like the one I've had in nearly thirty-seven years of recovery.

It does things to you if you actually experience your deepest fears and they turn out to be not so bad – indeed, it turns out to be a mind-bending grace. In recovery I've become almost fearless. I'm still afraid of heights and failure, of course, but my fears don't control me. When I can't sleep, I don't think it's because I'm afraid of dying; it's more that I'm afraid that lack of sleep may make me too cranky to help people.

But my fearlessness is about more than having had my worst fears come true without leaving permanent damage. It's also because I don't fear that death will find me disappointed or unsatisfied. I share this trait with a lot of people in recovery. What we most wanted in life, we have gotten from life. In fact, if we have been in recovery a while, we have gotten it repeatedly and on a grand scale.

NO MO FOMO

Raymond Carver found this at the end of his life. He had had a tumultuous writer's life, full of drinking and brawling, and then had stopped drinking for the last decade or so of that life before his death of cancer at 50. The last, brief work in his collected poems (*All of Us*) was, I believe, found in his desk after his death. At any rate it goes by the title *Late Fragment*. He asks himself if he got what he wanted from life "even so" – even though he was dying at fifty, thus ending a supportive second marriage, and just as his work was becoming more and more celebrated around the world. He answers, simply, "I did." He follows that up with a second question: What did he want from life, then? The answer: "To call myself beloved, to feel myself / beloved on the earth."

There are depths in this laconic epitaph. Carver doesn't simply say, "to be loved," but "to call myself beloved," and then "to feel myself beloved," in that order. It's one thing to speak of being loved, but so often our speech is belied by our actions, especially when alcohol is in the picture. But Carver also feels this love, which can be a rare privilege, especially if you have ferociously demanded love, and then thrown it away if you received it, as alcoholics do.

I don't think Carver was saying that all he wanted was to be loved, but that he couldn't be bothered about loving other people. In *Twelve Steps and Twelve Traditions*, Bill Wilson's commentary on the AA program that he helped to shape, he lists eight satisfactions that the recovering person can expect from working the AA program. One of these is "the proof that love freely given surely brings a full return" (124). Bill says this near the end of his commentary on the 12th and last Step, by way of *Farewell Words to the Fellowship.* A statement like this would be received with bitter scorn by someone in active addiction, and by a lot of other people as well. But for people in recovery, it's a Promise—not only are we told that this will happen, but most of us will readily agree that it's happened to us over and over. I hope that many people are finding this satisfaction amid the small but potent gestures that they are making at this time of great sickness.

Carver ends his little farewell with "on this earth." It's only on the earth, where things like pandemics occur, that human beings also find ways to sing to and greet one another even in the middle of a world-wide sickness. Robert Frost, another craggy poet, made the same point, in his wry New England way: "Earth's the right place for love; /I don't know where it's likely to go better" (*Birches*). One of my Jesuit brothers said the other day that when the pandemic first hit, he wanted to run away to a sunnier place than the gray Northwest where he and I live. He's from southern California, after all. But of course there's no place to run: the virus is everywhere. And if love is going to happen, it's only going to happen here – on this earth, the only place where, as far as we know, human beings live and can flourish.

I think Carver is right to reduce his wants to loving and being loved. I for one don't have a bucket list. The first morning I woke up sober, in a detox ward, my first thought was that now I could go to England. Although as I've mentioned I am an expert on British novels, I had never been to England: I was afraid that I might not have the necessary booze available at all times (and yes, that may have been an absurd fear, given pubs and other British institutions). Now, if this crazy recovery process worked, I could go to England, or indeed any place in the world. Even now, all these years later, I still haven't been to England; but I've been to Thailand and Sweden and Ireland, and didn't have to hunt for booze in any of them.

But the real point is that what I really wanted – not stamps on a visa or various kinds of honors or achievements – was what Carver wanted, and what I think we all want – to believe that we can be, and are, loved. If you have experienced that, the rest is, to cite another late poem of Carver's, *Gravy*.

BAD DREAMS AND SPIRITUAL AWAKENING

I've known people whose deaths were very hard because they seemed to be devoured by the idea that they hadn't gotten what they wanted, or, more painfully, what they were entitled to get. Sometimes these people have been surrounded by people who cared about them, but it seemed like the dying person couldn't see them. Perhaps they couldn't because they were in the throes of a dream.

This is something that recovering gambling addicts taught me. They speak of "the dream world of the gambling addict." These gamblers can't stop focusing on the big win that will finally make all their dreams come true, and thus make the rest of us stop criticizing them for their gambling. Gamblers are like a lot of people: They don't want to be loved as much as they want to be proved right. Of course their dream never comes true, because the house always wins.

So you have the melancholy tableau of someone dying miserable because they can't wake up and see the love that surrounds them. This is what happens to Willy Loman, the salesman, at the end of the great American tragedy, *Death of a Salesman*: He kills himself to give his son Biff the insurance money to realize that American dream to which Willy has sacrificed his life, even though Biff has just agonizingly told Willy that he loves him, and that the dream is deadly.

I believe that recovering people taught me early enough in my life about the things worth seeking that I have long since stopped wasting time trying to realize other aspirations. Anyone who participates in recovery groups with any energy knows in their bones that they are loved. And if you know that, then death doesn't get to be proud.

So I have never been very interested in the question of why God – or a "Higher Power," to use a preferred term of recovering people – allows things like pandemics, allows dozens of elderly people to die in one nursing home. What matters to me is the love with which we can meet the disaster. "Earth's the right place for love": The only reason to have lived, to have been on the earth, is to have known love. I once did a funeral for a little girl who was born with a terrible neurological disease. It was known from the first that she would not live long. But not a single person at that funeral, after she died at three or four, felt like she had missed anything essential. She had loved people fiercely, and we all knew it.

Jewish people use the Yiddish word "mensch" to describe someone like this. Although it comes from the German word for "man," it can also mean "human being." But it means much more than that. A "mensch" is someone who is "just," which in the Hebrew Scriptures means someone who treats everyone rightly. In the end, you could translate "justice" in this special sense by "love."

I could easily have missed my chance to be a mensch, although that's really a title that other people give you – you don't bestow it on yourself. Or, to put it more simply, I could have missed the chance to know myself loved on the earth. To practice an addiction is to know you've cut yourself off from the world of loving – that world Wendell Berry describes when he says that "love moves in a bright sphere." When active addicts speak of love, they are mostly lying. For example, in addict-speech, "I love you" really means "I may behave lovingly toward you if you help me get my drug, but whatever you do, don't keep me from it."

Recovering people chant "Keep coming back [to meetings]: We'll love you until you can love yourself." They could say further "We'll love you until you can love other people again." I have found this to be true for me. And since I have been able to love for all these recovering years, I will not meet death feeling that I have missed anything essential. Sure, I never married and I never had children of my own. I could have been a miserable old incel despite my public role of being a priest. But with the help of a group of loving addicts, I have known, I think, the one essential experience for human beings.

IT'S KIND OF A FUNNY STORY

And that is why I have to laugh a lot. I have gotten by, metaphorically, with murder. Less metaphorically, I was well on the way to committing slow suicide, to living a life without love, but then I stumbled into "a solution," and "something vastly more than that" (*Big Book*, 25, 152). Something that killed most of my older male relatives, something that embittered life on both sides of my family, that something happened to me, and it ended up by doing me a world of good. That's pretty funny if you think about it.

Of course, "some [may] be shocked at our seeming worldliness and levity" (*Big Book*, 16). As a recovering priest, I laugh a lot and like it when other people laugh with me, but some frown on this approach. They don't think there's anything funny about alcoholism, or about religion either.

For instance, a couple in a parish where I worked were coming up on their fiftieth wedding anniversary and wanted a ceremony to mark the occasion. They hit "reply all," I hope inadvertently, on a message in which they specified that they didn't want me to do that ceremony, because the husband didn't want "Milton Berle" involved.

I did not react well; I assured them that we could find a more lugubrious priest to do the honors, to which the wife replied that I shouldn't be offended – there were probably plenty of people in the parish who (shallow people as they were) thoroughly enjoyed me. I let the matter go then – I didn't come roaring back, for example, that people who knew who Milton Berle was were not exactly hip.

Instead, what I'd say about it now is that they were right, I do laugh a lot in my work. How can I keep from laughing, since the essence of comedy is having things turn out in a way that's so surprising that it rearranges your rigid categories? Comedy happens when you go to great lengths to hide from something and it sneaks up behind you, bites you on the ass, and saves your life. Anyway, that's the story of my life, and I hope you find it as funny as I do.

The only way we'll get through this pandemic is love, with a laughter chaser. Yes, we're going to cry, but there will have to be moments when the unexpected blessings that fall on our heads make us fall about laughing.

Tom Robbins, that gonzo Northwestern novelist, once said in his cannabis-scented novel *Even Cowgirls Get the Blues* that the only things human beings have really created are "kissing and comedy." Then he adds, "And by God that's enough." We have been given "by God" these two great gifts, and have been creative enough to use them and improve on them. Even in a time of social distancing, they will get us to the other side. We may not be able to imagine a lot of what's on the other side of the pandemic, but let's presume that there will continue to be "kissing and comedy." Won't that be better than the hatred and violence of the last few years?

Chapter 2

❧

No Greater Love

So I don't think I'm afraid of dying, because I've known some good loving. But I'm also complying with suggestions from experts that I take precautions because I'm old. At least here in Washington, where the pandemic surfaced first in the United States, most of my contemporaries are doing the same, to judge from the phone conversations I've had with the elders of my parish.

But there are minority voices who take a different view. This has been briskly summarized on the Internet as Lay Down Your Life for the Economy: The idea is that older people should go shopping more to strengthen the economy while the stock market continues to slide, and if they get sick and die, it's worth it. Some would go further and call the Covid-19 pandemic The Boomer Remover: In addition to helping the economy, old people would benefit society by contracting the illness, shrinking their numbers, and leaving more space for young people.

LAYING DOWN YOUR LIFE FOR MAMMON

Why do I disagree with this view, since I have claimed that I'm not afraid of death? Indeed, I would be willing to "lay down my life" in certain circumstances. If I were called to give Catholic sacraments to someone with the virus, I would of course go, although I would mask up and gown up and abide by other requirements at the facility or home I went to. I've always done this as part of my work as a priest. So I am willing to "lay down my life." After all, this phrase is spoken by Jesus at the Last Supper in the Gospel of John: What he actually says is "Greater love than this no one has than to lay down one's life for one's friends." And he says this a few hours before he does just that, so we know he isn't theorizing.

In fact, many of the people to whom I have given the sacraments for the very ill were people I had never met before, so "friends" here can be taken to mean "any human being who needs what I have." This has long been the inclusive understanding of "friends" in Christian circles: St. Aloysius Gonzaga, a Jesuit who came from a noble Italian family, died of the plague after caring for the infected, and there have been many more like him. This is similar to the inclusiveness practiced by 12 Step fellowships. One of the 12 Traditions, the principles that shape 12 Step groups (the Steps are for the individuals making up the groups), makes the entrance requirements as minimal as possible. In AA, for example, "the only requirement . . . is a desire to stop drinking."

But laying down one's life for the economy? This would make "the economy" into a Higher Power; in the Gospels, this Higher Power even has a name, Mammon, and Jesus says some mysterious things about Mammon. For that matter, whatever you call it, "the economy" has always figured largely in people's minds. You might think that Marxism and capitalism are total opposites, but both of them center on "the economy."

SCROOGE AND THE PANDEMIC
Both Marxism and capitalism, or at least one form of capitalism, began in 19th Century England, one of the first

societies to industrialize on the basis of large capital investments and of exploiting workers. And in my studies of 19th Century English fiction, I came across a work that takes up this question of "laying down one's life." This is far from an unknown tale: it's Charles Dickens's *A Christmas Carol*, which dates from 1843.

There have been many stage and screen adaptations of Dickens's story over the years. Indeed, it was so popular that people were putting it on stage within days of its coming out in print. Many, perhaps most of these adaptations, soft-pedal some of Dickens's critique of what was known back then as "political economy." The spokesman for "political economy" in this tale is the central character, Ebenezer Scrooge. At the beginning, in his counting house, he is solicited by some do-gooders to contribute to Christmas "welfare" for the less fortunate. You'll recall that he flatly refuses, and in fact states, following the ideas of Thomas Malthus, that it would be a good thing if poor people died, because it would decrease the "surplus population."

Later, after Scrooge is shown the home of his worker, Bob Cratchit, and especially his frail son, Tiny Tim, Scrooge's heart begins to awaken after a long paralysis. But when he asks if Tiny Tim can be saved, a Spirit flings his words about the "surplus population" in his teeth. Only in the last words of *A Christmas Carol* does the narrator assure us that "Tiny Tim did not die." But of course he doesn't die because Scrooge, a wealthy man, underwent a change of heart. What about all the other frail children of Victorian England, underfed, living in the most polluted city in the world?

Imagine a version of Dickens's work for our time. It would center on, let's say, a pundit, one of the people who bluntly stated that old people should go shopping. The Spirit of Easter Present might take this commentator to a nursing home. The *New York Times* did just that in a story about the nursing home in suburban Seattle where the pandemic began. It focused, among others, on a particular 90-year-old woman. She had always been feisty and upbeat, and helped the other residents to deal with the difficulties of their lives. After she became ill with the virus, she could only interact with her family through closed windows and by phone. When she knew she was going to die, she said good-bye to her loved ones and forbade them to come to her bedside, even though they could have under these circumstances. She died alone, protecting them from her illness. She laid down her life for them.

Her death can't be brutally reduced to "laying down her life for the economy." How can the pundits and politicos of our time be as hard- hearted as Scrooge? Would it touch their hearts if they could watch one actual old woman who died of Covid?

LAYING DOWN YOUR LIFE FOR EVOLUTION

As it happens, after Scrooge's time another set of ideas helped to further harden the hearts of economists. Sixteen years after *A Christmas Carol*, another Victorian writer published a landmark work: Charles Darwin's *The Origin of Species*.

It's important to distinguish Darwin's original ideas, which Pope Francis studied thoughtfully in his encyclical *Laudato Si*, from the way those ideas were later popularized and distorted. In the later 19th and earlier 20th Century, in England and elsewhere, especially the United States, Darwin's concept of natural selection, "the survival of the fittest" in its pop version, became the central focus of Social Darwinism. The idea here was that evolution could use a helping hand to accomplish its improvement of the human species.

First, of course, it was important to decide which kinds of humans were more evolved, and imperialist racism came in handy. White Northern Europeans decided that white Northern Europeans were the most evolved, which left out everyone else. And among white Northern Europeans, the "fittest" were the young, strong, straight, and "normally" intelligent. And this left out the old, the weak, the "other," and those who were dismissed as "imbeciles." I use this ugly word because the Chief Justice of the United States Supreme Court, Oliver Wendell Holmes, used it in a 1927 decision upholding the rights of states to involuntarily sterilize people alleged to be of sub-normal intelligence. He said that two generations of "imbeciles" were enough.

Perhaps it's no surprise to learn that the woman in the case on which Justice Holmes ruled was not in fact of "sub-normal" intelligence, and that she was from Virginia, where the statute was particularly applied to multi-racial people. What may be surprising is that Social Darwinism was a very widely held belief, and not just by supreme haters like Adolf Hitler; it was quite popular with "sophisticated," "progressive" people all over the world.

So the notion, all over the Internet in early March, that old people are expendable in an effort to shore up the economy, had some pretty deep roots in the Euro-American past that Americans are always so ready to forget. At times of crisis, people often regress to what 12 Steppers call "old ideas," the lethal, destructive beliefs that it has cost so many lives to defeat – racism, "eugenics," white supremacy, ethnic cleansing, demonizing of people by age or ethnicity. At a moment like ours, we need instead to turn to what Abraham Lincoln called "the better angels of our natures." The unimaginable world after this virus – and before the next one? – needs to be shaped by "better angels," not the kind of primitive fake truths that have so dominated our public discourse in the last few years.

TRIAGE

One more lesson from the wonderful woman in the nursing home.

She did not refuse to lay down her life – but she did it

for those she loved, not for Mammon. Difficult medical decisions like the one she made are necessary during this pandemic, and not just where there is a shortage of essential medical equipment. An especially harsh form of triage is occurring these days.

This topic has also been canvassed in the responsible press. It goes back to Napoleon's army, and has been practiced, in war and peace, all over the world since. It has to be practiced wherever there is a greater medical need than can be met with available resources. It has been essential, for example, in deciding who receives transplants of scarce, vital organs.

The tri- in "triage," originally a French word, suggests a division of casualties into three groups: one group can be set aside until later and still stand a good chance of recovering; one group is beyond help, and can only be treated with palliative care; the third group consists of those who will respond well to whatever medical efforts are available. There are of course infinite shadings within these categories.

We have been told from the first that Covid-19 is especially lethal for older people with underlying conditions like diabetes and heart disease.

Today hundreds of decisions are being made across the world about people ill with the virus: Which of them are more likely to survive on a ventilator? Which of them are failing to recover, even with a ventilator? This is very different from telling old people to go shopping and never mind the consequences.

The old woman in the nursing home did triage on herself. She knew that she was probably not going to survive. But she also chose not to expose her loved ones to the virus, even though that made her death lonelier. I hope that her dying was at the same time softened by the knowledge of the gift she had given in her passing.

DYING AND RECOVERY

I have witnessed the deaths of recovering people, and have participated in their memorials. There is often an ease in dying for them, and a deep sense of gratitude in the loved ones they leave behind, because the recovering people have laid down their lives for so many people. They did this in the most practical way: they formed their lives into a story that they told other recovering people. And the whole secret of recovery is that a story well-told, of a life well and lovingly lived, gives life, saves life.

This is why I think I would be ready and able to let my life go, in this pandemic or some other circumstance: I found my story long ago, and have told it again and again, and have seen the healing that came from it. Early in the pandemic I called a recently recovering person and learned that he was thinking of drinking; I said that I was, too, and that a whole lot of recovering alcoholics had probably considered a drink at this hard time. I laid down my life for him to consider. We talked after that about a lot of things; and we've talked repeatedly since. And so far neither of us has had to drink.

In the new world after the pandemic, people will, I think, continue to lay down their lives for the right things – for love, for life, for grandchildren. I hope that one of the ways to tell the post-pandemic world from the world we're leaving behind will be that more people will have learned the lesson of the woman in the nursing home and of all the other people who are making heart-rending sacrifices at this terrible time.

Chapter 3

❧❧

Edgar Allan Poe at the Gun Shop

I n the last few weeks, people have been comparing this pandemic to some of the great literary depictions of past outbreaks. Alain de Botton had a piece in Sunday's *New York Times* reflecting on Albert Camus' *The Plague*, written in the 1940s and set in North Africa. De Botton made the point that what Camus argues in his novel is that the plague is not an allegory for fascism or for any other evil that comes and goes.

Camus' point rather is the existential idea that "the plague" we have is always with us.

In the Jesuit poet Gerard Manley Hopkins' words, it "is the blight man was born for" (*Spring and Fall: To a Young Child*). Something large and dark is always going to be rising above the human horizon. We may deny it, run from it, distract ourselves from it, meanly try to make sure that it affects the underclass, not us. But it is always too great.

Only by changing our hearts one by one and then uniting our changed hearts in life-saving efforts can we respond meaningfully to "the plague."

Other pundits have referenced another great plague story in trying to come to terms with our pandemic, Edgar Allan Poe's *The Masque of the Red Death*, written a hundred years before Camus' novel. Poe struggled with alcohol and other drugs throughout his life, and died under circumstances that have never been fully explained: he disappeared, apparently on some kind of drug-fueled binge, and was found disoriented on the streets of Baltimore a few days later. He died without fully regaining his senses.

Perhaps an addiction narrative peeps out in Poe's story. He tricks it out in fancy outfits, setting it in a quasi-medieval castle where a blue-blooded costume ball is going on among some aristocrats who believe they have escaped the plague by holing up in a castle, like the characters in Boccaccio's *Decameron*. But a red-masked guest shows up and proceeds inexorably through the castle, slowly harvesting the guests with the signature bleeding of the plague (as in pneumonic plague, as a matter of fact). Unlike Hollywood horror movies, there are no survivors at the end of Poe's story, no Final Girl (or Boy). Like addiction, the Red Death seems to be inexorable. And the worst thing is, the harder you try to escape it, the surer you are to find it.

THE GUN SHOP

Poe's lurid scenario sheds some practical light on the way some people have behaved since the outbreak of Covid-19. Many have acted irrationally or futilely, like the aristocrats in the castle – no surprise given how terrifying these times are. For instance, sales of guns and applications for background checks for guns have soared.

If we were to do a modern version of Poe's story, it might run like this:

Frightened by the news of the outbreak, a small group buys a lot of guns and retreats to its safe room. There they await their panic-stricken neighbors, armed with torches and pitchforks, coming as a crazed mob for the survivalists' toilet paper. But what happens is that the virus was on the counter of the gun shop when they were examining the weapons they went there to buy. They brought the virus back with them, and it has been in their safe room from the beginning. There it slowly passes from one of them to another. So how will their guns help them as they sicken? They will not need firepower; they will need someone else's unimaginable compassion.

Fortunately, it turns out in our days that there is as much compassion out there as there is firepower. The people to admire at a time like this are figures like the doctor who is the central character in Camus' novel. Along with the narratives of panic, as well as the efforts of con artists, including religious leaders and politicians, to get people to fall for bogus cures, along with the demonizing of groups or countries, we have plenty of counter-narratives of people showing up at the greatest risk to care for the sick.

FR. DAMIEN LAYS DOWN HIS LIFE

There have always been people who found the enormous courage, the love, to do things like this. Think of Fr. Damien. A Belgian priest, he traveled in the late 19th

Century to the lepers on the island of Molokai, part of Hawaii. Since then we have learned a lot more about Hansen's disease, which is what we now call this sickness. Surprisingly, it is not that contagious: a complex combination of internal as well as external factors causes someone exposed to it to contract it. And in the 20th Century medications were discovered that could control its effects. But of course Fr. Damien didn't know all that when he got himself rowed to the largely inaccessible shore of Molokai. He just felt that God was calling him to minister to these people, many of them indigenous, cut off from their families for life.

In taking this step – and he was roundly criticized, then and later, by church authorities for doing so – Fr. Damien believed that he was imitating his Higher Power, whom he called Jesus Christ. He was canonized a few years ago, so his hunch has now been officially approved.

Even a cursory reading of the Gospels will make clear that Jesus too took a brave and loving stand toward "lepers." If Fr. Damien was making a leap in the dark, Jesus was making one from an even higher board. Jewish beliefs about leprosy, as spelled out especially in the book of Leviticus in the Hebrew Scriptures, were much harsher than the ideas that shaped the colony on Molokai.

JESUS TOUCHES LEPERS

As is usually the case when a society is dealing with a problem which it really understands very little, the strictures of Leviticus were mainly guesswork. First of all, "leprosy" was their term for any skin ailment. The only way in which "leprosy" could be distinguished from an ordinary zit was that the zit would go away in a fairly short time. Any skin problem that persisted was "leprosy." And there was of course no way of knowing what caused the problem, no knowledge of contagion, any more than people knew about disease-carrying agents during the Black Death of the 14th Century or the cholera epidemics that swept through London during the 19th.

So if you had a skin problem that persisted, to be on the safe side, Jesus's society would quarantine you. You could have no contact with anyone except for other people with "leprosy"; you would live in particularly unsanitary conditions that would necessarily worsen whatever your illness was. You would, in other words, have to live like homeless people live in the United States, and you would have to warn people away by announcing your condition.

Of course the skin problems of some sufferers would eventually go away for an unknown reason – it would just take longer than a zit. In that case, according to Leviticus, you could be certified "clean" again, curiously enough by a priest. Yes, the assumption that someone with "leprosy" was religiously unclean would arise naturally in this worldview, and a religious process would be necessary for the person to officially rejoin society.

In the Gospels, Jesus repeatedly encountered "lepers." They typically asked him for healing; in fact they had already violated community rules by coming close enough to Jesus to make their request. They didn't maintain "social distancing." Jesus in turn broke the rules by touching them. Nobody knew whether he would get "it" by that contact, any more than we know whether there is coronavirus on the motorized black plastic strip that you put your groceries on. But in any event he was breaking The Rules by reaching out, whatever the result.

The way the world is reacting to Covid-19 is like the way the world reacts to anything mysterious and frightening and different. It's similar to the way the world reacted to HIV when it surfaced in the 1980s. But it's not just a question of diseases; any kind of difference can lead to demonizing and quarantining.

LORD, I AM NOT WORTHY

Jesus was also remarkable for his willingness to interact with Gentiles, people not part of his ethnic group.

There's a story, often misinterpreted, in which he encounters a Gentile military officer, who asks Jesus to cure his servant. Jesus is willing to go to the officer's house to see the sick person, but the officer considerately says, "You don't have to do that. I am not worthy. I know enough about Judaism to know that being in my house would be distasteful to you, that it might render you religiously 'tainted.' But as a military man, I know how power works: so just send an order for him to be healed."

The centurion shows exquisite courtesy in saying he is not "worthy"; by "worthy" he simply means "not socially acceptable." People are wrong to understand "worthy" in moral terms. In his turn, Jesus greatly praises the man's "faith," and in fact contrasts it with the attitudes of his fellow Jews to his message. If this story were happening now, the servant might have Covid-19; in this modern version the officer would tell Jesus not to risk infection by coming to his house. Instead he would suggest that Jesus can – somehow – cure the servant from a distance.

I'm not suggesting, as some Christian ministers are now, that an appeal to Jesus – through these ministers – can cure the virus. What we can imitate is Jesus's willingness to run risks in rendering service, and the centurion's willingness to observe social distancing. We can also do something that wasn't possible in Jesus's time: we can cross distances with computers and smartphones and the whole array of technological devices. Sending love electronically is not a cure, but it's a great help, not just to people with the virus, but to the many more people who are agonizing over the long-term social and economic effects of it.

ELECTRONIC TOUCHING

There has been much debate about social media and the other communication devices that have appeared in the current generation. Do they isolate us, distract us, harden our hearts, make us more rigid about the beliefs of our social niche? Now, in the face of the pandemic, we can see that, along with the baleful effects of media, they can also produce great good.

I have been anything but a quick adapter of the new technology. But I have to admit that it is saving my sanity these days. I work at a parish in Tacoma, St. John of the Woods, whose members I love with all my heart.

The Catholic Church in Western Washington was one of the first to close churches to limit the risk of infection. And of course no recovery meetings can take place now: as it happens, I tend to favor meetings that take place in church basements, and churches were some of the first spaces to close. What's happening instead is that I am in touch via Zoom meetings with people who mean the world to me. And I am doing what I only learned to do in the second half of my life, after I found recovery: I am empathizing with them, offering comfort, making them laugh, pointing to a hopeful future.

Why did it take me so long to find this solution to the pain of the world? Well, first because I'm far from a naturally optimistic person. I'm half-German and half-Irish, and these are not typically cheery people. Then, too, it took me a while to understand and to deploy the gifts I was given at birth. It's not always easy to tell the difference between a feature and a bug. In Al-Anon, Steps 4 and 5 are about traits, which may be defects, but may also be assets if you look at them and use them in the right way.

IN THE BEGINNING WAS THE WORD

My most obvious gift is words. I know a lot of them. Some of them are in languages other than English: in high school and college I had eight years of Latin and six years of Greek. I love to play with words. Of course you will note that two of my specialties are dead languages, so for me words are not necessarily about communicating with other people. I may prefer just to play with them in my room, alone with my cat who stubbornly refuses to learn English.

Like a lot of gifts, the gift of words has to be grown into. My birthday is at the end of October. My parents decided that I should start kindergarten before I turned five. Ever since then I have warned other parents to wait a year: when I began school, I was intellectually advanced and emotionally delayed, and I think that remained true for much of my life. I knew what a lot of words meant, but I didn't know how they felt. I had learned the words out of books, not out of interaction with other people.

I had to learn along the way to use words to help other people.

Words, like character traits, can go either way: they can help and comfort and support, but they can also be used to hurt. Like most fat, bright boys, I was bullied; like most of these boys, I learned to use the weapons I had to bully others. A lot of my 8th and 9th Steps were about this.

It's been a long and slow process. What helped more than anything was stories. One of the reasons why I loved words and learned so many at an early age was that I wanted access to stories, and they are made entirely of words. In my hunger for stories, when I was about five I read a long-forgotten, bawdy novel about cats and baseball called *Rhubarb*. It includes a scene where a couple get drunk and end up in bed together, covered with spaghetti. When I read this, all I learned about was spaghetti. Everything else this couple did I filed with the other incomprehensible things that grown-ups do.

When I later came down with alcoholism, it seemed to me a great blessing that recovery mostly involved the sharing of stories. There's nothing I like better anyway, and this sharing had the added benefit of saving and changing my life.

So that is why I am writing and telling stories in the middle of a pandemic. I know that stories help people, and, like the great short story artist Flannery O'Connor, I think telling stories is what I was made for. She once said that people where surprised when she told them why she wrote. She thought they expected her to say that she wrote to glorify God (she was a practicing Catholic) or to show the possibilities of the short story form. No, she answered: she wrote because she was really good at it. I am writing this because Annie Lamott supports my private belief that I am good at stories. Even in the early days of the pandemic in the United States, there were poems and blessings and reflections on the Internet from people who were sending out words and stories to help us all get through this. Everybody is using whatever gifts they have; words are mine.

Chapter 4

❧

Felix Culpa

The topic of gifts brings me to a question that some religious leaders – priests, ministers, rabbis, imams – have been attempting to wrestle with online: Why is the pandemic happening? What role, if any, does God as they understand God have in these dire events?

WHY THE PANDEMIC?

Some pastors on the Internet are only too happy to give an answer to this question; they round up the Usual Suspects, and say that God is so upset with them that God sent the virus to show God's thorough disapproval of them. But the underlying idea here – God has the same resentments that I do – is pretty dangerous for recovering people. We are strongly urged to live in a way that isn't fueled by resentments, because such a life makes it hard to move beyond our addictions. If God is so angry at "defective" people, why would God want to help addicts – whose defections are on a majestic scale – get better?

People who want a more searching answer to why bad

things happen to good people have a lot of wise people whom they can consult. One of the wisest is Rabbi Harold Kushner, who wanted to know why his only son, Aaron, had progeria, that terrible disease that ages children and ends their young lives.

DO GOOD THINGS COME OUT OF BAD THINGS?

You can read the rabbi's heartfelt book on this subject, *When Bad Things Happen to Good People.* My own answer relies on an old Christian notion, expressed in the title of this chapter. *Felix culpa* is a phrase from a prayer that is said, or more precisely chanted, on the most solemn night of the Christian year of worship. It is sung on the night before Easter, after sundown. It hails the coming dawn of Easter as a symbol of what Easter celebrates, the resurrection of Jesus.

It comes from a prayer called the *Exsultet* (Latin for "let [the church] rejoice"). Like the *Dayenu* prayer said at the Jewish Seder, it's a gratitude list, a prayer that blesses God for all the gifts that come with Easter. The particular phrase *felix culpa* occurs in the context of a reflection on the Fall of Adam and Eve, the Biblical notion that something is broken in this beautiful world, and that human beings have something to do with that brokenness. If we were speaking of Covid-19, we might see it as a sign of the Fall, in the sense that human beings have foolishly abused the environment, and the pandemic is one result.

The cantor chants that we are grateful because God has turned out to be more powerful than our human ineptitude. The new life that Jesus is said to bring is not just for human beings; it is for all of creation. St. Paul says that creation has been "groaning" along with humanity because of all the wretchedness in the world, and that creation will in the end rejoice when a better world arrives. Easter is a festival of new life, which is why in popular celebration it includes eggs and bunnies.

At this point the cantor chants that the fault – *culpa* –

of Adam and Eve and all their offspring – is in the end *felix*
– happy – because it has been the occasion for the
outbreaking of new life in the world. It's a powerful
paradox that covers the same ground as the ordinary idea
that good can come out of evil. But when this happens, it
feels as if something has occurred way beyond what our
human efforts might achieve.

GOOD THINGS LIKE THE PROMISES

Think of this as a Promise, like the Promises in the *Big
Book*. One of those Promises captures this idea pretty well:
God is doing for us what we could not do for ourselves.
Recovering persons notice that they suddenly have the
power, not just to forgo their addictive behavior, but to be
content forgoing it. When we're practicing our addictions,
we keep wistfully hoping that we will "somehow, someday
. . . control and enjoy [our] drinking (BB 30)." We cannot
"imagine life either with alcohol or without it" (BB 152).
And then a more imaginative – a "higher" – power
introduces us to a life without alcohol but with
contentment, a combination that would never have
seemed to us possible or desirable.

This is new life, "a new freedom and a new happiness"
(another Promise, BB 83). What *felix culpa* suggests is that
all the misery of our addictions was somehow necessary to
produce the raw materials for this new life—another
Promise, "We will not regret the past nor wish to shut the
door on it" (BB 83). How can we regret something that
mysteriously brought us to this new life?

The *Big Book* captures this paradox well. Chapter 9,
"The Family Afterwards," has this version of the *felix culpa*:
"The alcoholic's past thus becomes the principal asset of
the family and frequently it is almost the only one!" (124),
and "When we see [someone] sinking into the mire that is
alcoholism, we give [them] first aid and place what we
have at [their] disposal. For [their] sake, we do recount
and almost relive the horrors of our past" (132). For an

alcoholic, the culpa is "the horrors of our past." Central to recovery, as Chapter 5 says, is honestly facing those horrors, and taking responsibility for our part in them. But through a spiritual alchemy, the "horrors" are turned into an "asset," a path to new life, something *felix*, a fellowship of people who can "laugh[ ] at their own misfortunes and underst[an]d" (160) the misfortunes of the newcomer.

THE MAGIC OF STORIES

Once again, this alchemy is accomplished with the simplest of means: we reshape those "horrors" into a story, and a story which, looked at in a new perspective, is kind of funny. Comedy often involves a clown doing the same foolish thing over and over and never learning anything from the disastrous results, a kind of mechanical movement like a puppet's or a toon's. What happens in recovery is that the puppet becomes a real boy or girl again, and begins to do different, more rewarding things. Toons never age: Bart Simpson is still a bratty boy, thirty years later. Recovering people have re-entered time, and can grow and change, a process that was halted when the addiction took over.

My hunch and my hope is that something similar is occurring and will continue as we live through the pandemic. We are all hungry for stories these days, stories about gallant people like the woman in the nursing home. Through all the media available to us, we hunt for news about people like a recovering friend of mine who is doing emergency dental care for people with the virus. Or like a nurse, the daughter of another friend, who has had the virus and is going back to work believing that she is now immune and can especially help the infected. Or Drew Brees and his wife: he is the long-time quarterback of the New Orleans Saints, and together they have given five million dollars to help their city weather the pandemic.

I don't know why the pandemic is happening. But the story of the response of some people to it can only be called godly, since it goes so far beyond what we ordinarily think of as human behavior. It makes me want to be better than I am, and sometimes these days that is what happens, when I call someone with a message of hope or help someone to a much-needed laugh.

And we were needing a call to be better than ourselves, in the face of so many events that have portrayed us at our worst. For every person who has shot up a shopping mall or a place of worship, we need a lot of people bravely doing their jobs to erase the scars on our psyches.

STORIES AND GRATITUDE

Some recovering people describe themselves as "grateful alcoholics." This can take some getting used to, until you grasp the concept of the "happy fault." It would be glib to say we should be, or someday will be, grateful for the pandemic. But even now we can begin to be grateful for the nobility that some people have shown in dealing with it. That nobility is something we will need badly in the new world on the other side of the pandemic.

One more item under the heading of *felix culpa*: for a long time, as I mentioned before, it has been fashionable to decry the various forms of social media that have multiplied like locusts in our times. I have been far from an early adapter of most technological advances. To this day I haven't gone on Facebook or Twitter – which are by now very old hat, in fact – because I felt guilty about not keeping up even with "primitive" message systems like phone calls and emails.

We have all heard, and perhaps repeated, the usual critiques: that all the electronic media distract us and isolate us, numb us to the real pain that people experience, and eat up time. Some have gone so far as to diagnose addiction in the case of some people's use of video games. I believe there are even 12 Step programs to help people with these problems.

All of this was true in the World Before the Pandemic, which now looks to be as unrecoverable as the world of *Downton Abbey* or the Happy Family (alleged) era of the American 1950s. But, as I noted above, what has in fact happened, and in a breathtakingly brief period of time, is that recovery meetings have adjourned wholesale to online programs like Zoom. And what a blessing – how *felix* – these programs have turned out to be.

Not only is it possible for people sheltering at home to participate fully in meetings, both with sight and sound; but people from across the country, or even the world, people who used to attend a particular meeting and then moved, or people thousands of miles away who are looking for a meeting, can all participate with the push of a button – especially if they're quarantined with an eight-year-old of average intelligence who can show them which button to push. At a time when a lot of addicts are struggling to stay in recovery, and a lot of non-addicts are struggling to keep their wits about them, you can see and talk to someone who's working through the same temptations and the same fears. "Carrying the message" of recovery has never been so easy, or so far-reaching. Early members of the 12 Step programs would be astonished at what we can so easily do to work the 12th Step.

Finally, online 12 Step meetings and online religious services are providing another wonderful benefit. We have these electronic substitutes for now, and they are a profound relief and a cure for isolation and the strange ideas that isolation breeds. A brief survey of the Internet will give you a taste of some very weird ideas that people not doing well emotionally are sharing.

But even more, the electronic meetings of groups dedicated to improving life and encouraging hope are also helping to build up a tremendous charge of love, a charge that will light up the new world on the other side of the pandemic. There's a 19th Century Anglican hymn about heaven that can be taken to describe what will happen when many church and 12 Step communities physically reunite when this hard time is over: "What knitting severed friendships up/ Where partings are no more!" In that new world we will knit up, with a long hug, the friendships that the virus "severed." The electronic meetings are a godsend; but there is a great longing for the Real Thing. Meanwhile, I for one promise never again to disdain the Internet or smartphones or any of the other gizmos in our lives: for all their faults, they are on balance a happy option.

Chapter 5

❧❦

Tomorrow

Today is Holy Thursday, April 9th. This is the day when many Christians wash the feet of others. Pope Francis does it his way: instead of choosing twelve high-ranking cardinals, he washes the feet of men and women in jail or in a homeless shelter, including immigrants and non-Catholics. In doing this, we are trying to imitate what Jesus is supposed to have done on the last night of his life. He and his disciples were gathered for a meal, a Seder according to Matthew, Mark, and Luke. In the Gospel of John, he washes the feet of the disciples.

FOOT-WASHING DAY

Disciples were supposed to do little, homely services for their rabbis, their guides in the study of sacred wisdom. But washing their rabbis' feet was considered too low even for a disciple. In a society without socks and without much paving, such a task was considered suitable only for the lowest servants, or, indeed, for slaves. So Jesus's gesture shocked them; Peter put his foot down (so to speak) and refused, until Jesus told him he had to submit to this.

The foot-washing ceremony of Holy Thursday is my favorite ritual gesture in the whole catalogue of rituals that occur in the course of the church's calendar. John the Evangelist thinks so highly of it that he doesn't even mention Jesus's blessing of bread and wine at the Last Supper, the source of the Lord's Supper, the Eucharist. John must think that the foot-washing says the same thing as the sharing of bread, and says it just as powerfully.

This year there can't be much washing off feet. I'd like to think that families or communities sheltered in their homes would enact this, but public re-enactments would be too risky with such a contagious virus around. So add foot-washing to the list of things that can't happen during this time of testing. Most Catholics can't even participate in the Eucharist now. Some nuns I know have chosen not to get blessed bread from elsewhere to share; they want to "fast" with all the non-ordained members of the church, which is noble, I think.

And of course other religious services and 12 Step meetings can only take place online; there can be no touching of loved ones outside of one's immediate family. This is just one of many deprivations, and like many people I want to know how long it will last. The answer of course is that no one knows.

THE PANDEMIC AND 'ONE DAY AT A TIME'

What do you do if you feel powerless and thoroughly dislike the way things are going in your life? This is a paraphrase of Step One, which says that we are powerless and our lives are unmanageable. Well, eleven steps follow this one, so there are things you can do to change this reality. But any change in depth, any spiritual change, takes time. For that matter, the change that is sought in the 12 Steps comes not from ourselves – it's not really "self-improvement" – but from power outside us, either the power of a group united for change, or the power of someone greater, or both. But since it's not our own power, we can't control the timetable, just as with Covid-19.

A spiritual practice I found very helpful from the beginning of my recovery is captured in the simple maxim "One Day at a Time." More than any of the other 12-Step slogans, this one spoke to me. Regret and anxiety figured largely in my drinking: I needed a break from worrying about substandard actions in the past and terrifying challenges in the future. As I've said, my drinker broke when I was trying to get a doctorate from one of the scariest institutions of higher learning in the United States. On any given day I would cringe at how badly I had done on the "Hundred Book Exam" because of my shaky background in literary criticism, or I would stop breathing at the thought of the "Three Area Exam" (I've forgotten the exact nickname) and – worst of all – the dissertation that I would somehow have to get through down the road.

Given this, it was a huge relief in early recovery to be able to focus just on today. I honestly had thought that grown-ups were forbidden to do this, which is why they aged so rapidly. The whole first year I was alcohol-free, I told myself that whatever I was feeling on a given day was what one feels in one's first year off the sauce, and that I only had to endure it for that day. One balmy summer day I went to bed at 7 p.m. because I couldn't bear another minute of that day, so I declared it over.

This practice has stood me, and other recovering people, in very good stead since the coronavirus crisis began. Looking back on it now, about six weeks into its Washington State version, it's amazing how many unimaginable changes have occurred in such a short time. We adjusted to this by taking each day and its new facts and regulations as they came.

Today we don't shake hands at Mass: OK. The next day

we Jesuits send only the youngest members of our
community out to buy food: good for them. Tomorrow
when I go to buy kitty litter for my cat, I'll wear a mask for
the first time: Luckily we were all issued one.

But even though it's better to take life, pandemic
included, a day at a time, it's natural to think from time to
time about life after it. As I write, some governors,
including ours here in Washington, are drafting plans for
what some people call "the re-opening." Interesting term:
much has had to be "closed" to save lives and to get us
through the pandemic, but a time will come when we will
be "open" again. Much of life is a matter of deciding when
and how much to be "open" to what comes: it's only
natural to clench when what is coming is painful, even if
the pain brings important lessons.

MONDEGREENS

Time for a tangent on mondegreens. You probably
haven't heard this term, and no, it has nothing to do with
Covid-19. A mondegreen occurs when you hear a song but
can't quite make out the lyrics, so you go around, perhaps
for years, singing along with your own grotesque version
of the lyrics. Mondegreen itself is a misheard version of
some lyric, although I have forgotten what the correct
words are.

I saw a collection of coffee mugs in a novelty store that
had some of the richest examples of this found poetry.
From the Eagles' "Hotel California": "On a dark desert
highway / Cool-Whip in my hair" (instead of "Cool wind in
my hair"). From the Beatles' "Lucy in the Sky with
Diamonds": "the girl with colitis goes by" (for "the girl with
kaleidoscope eyes"). One I came up with myself, from a
song called "I Fooled Around and Fell in Love" by Elvin
Bishop: I thought it was "Little Round Girls Fell in Love." Or
consider this: when the Go-Go's sang "Our Lips Are
Sealed," I thought they were saluting a little French-
Canadian girl named "Olive-Cecile."

I learned a year or two ago that I had committed a mondegreen on a song that means a lot to me, and to many other people as well: "That's What Friends Are For." It was written by Burt Bacharach and Carole Bayer Sager, and recorded by four towering artists: Elton John, Stevie Wonder, Gladys Knight, and Dionne Warwick. I believe that, when the song appeared in the late 1980s, it was so strongly associated with raising consciousness around the need for AIDS research that proceeds from the song went to that cause. You'll recall that those were the days during another pandemic when a diagnosis with a virus was in most cases a death sentence, and few medications had been developed to treat the virus or its symptoms.

Those were also the days when my brother Tim was diagnosed with HIV: like many then, he lived only two more years. In age we were two years apart in a family of six. When I got up to read at his memorial service in Las Vegas, there was a gasp from the congregation: most of them hadn't met me, and we looked so much alike. So for me "That's What Friends Are For" will always be about him.

The mondegreen appears around halfway through the song. I learned two years ago that the actual lyric is "Then you came in loving me / And now there's so much more I see. / And by the way I thank you." For twenty years before that I thought Elton John was singing "Then you came and opened me / And now there's so much more I see." I loved my mishearing because it reminded me of what Tim did for me, as a gay man, as someone with HIV, as someone neither deaf nor disabled who chose to work with children who were either: he opened me. And once I saw what he showed me, I never wanted to go back to being blind.

I was six years' sober when Tim died. In the reception line after his memorial service, one of his friends asked me how I was doing. I replied, "I've never felt worse, and I'm really grateful." I was grateful because I was open to the pain as it was happening. If I had still been drinking, I would have buried the pain in numbness for a later date.

THE WORLD AFTER THE PANDEMIC

So what will the "re-opening" be like after this Covid-19 plague (not that HIV is over; it's just much more treatable)? Many poems are circling on the Internet; it's surprising how moving and eloquent they are, but they all say pretty much the same thing: we are learning now, amid the pain, how much we mean to one another, how much we depend on other people, how important it is to bear one another's burdens at this time.

Last night I heard from a friend. He and his wife have three small daughters. His wife, a nurse, has volunteered to work in a unit for people with Covid-19. She brought home this story: a woman in the unit gave birth, a month premature. The mother is struggling with the virus; the baby cannot be held by either of its parents. Meanwhile my friend is caring for his and the nurse's daughters, since she cannot hold any of her own children while she works at saving lives.

As I write, I have family and friends praying for both couples and all the children involved. Now, in the middle of the pain, I don't know the outcome. But I do know that when the world reopens I will tell this story at religious services and during retreats. I hope fiercely that stories like this, remembered in that new world, will shape what is new about that world.

Many people have shared their wishes for the new world. Instead of trivial or degrading news items, we are being flooded with stories of courage, self-sacrifice, and generosity. These aren't necessarily new virtues, but they seemed to have gone underground in the past few years.

Instead, in the last several years we had been hearing about people like Ammon Bundy.

AMERICAN INDIVIDUALISM AND THE PANDEMIC

I feel for Mr. Bundy. He has a long history of anti-government demonstrations. A couple of weeks ago, he turned up in northern Idaho, exercised about orders to stay at home and not gather during the pandemic. He is single-mindedly dedicated to what has long been an American ideal: self-reliance. He doesn't want to depend on government or any other group except his own chosen few (he may well receive government support on the side, but let's skip that here).

What is sad about his beliefs and his efforts to implement them is that they are completely irrelevant to the virus. Self-reliance has no effect on a new virus; if you catch it and get very sick, you will be dependent on some brave medical people to get well. If someone you love catches it, you will be dependent on the same people to nurse them back to health. After a bout with it, you may develop an immunity to it, but that is not certain at this point.

No one knows in much detail what the world of tomorrow is going to be like. It dawned on most of us early in the pandemic that things were changing dramatically and irreversibly, but what would remain is a matter of hope, not certainty. We would like beautiful things to accompany us into the new world. Self-reliance doesn't even work in the world in transition, so it probably won't be helpful in the new world, and perhaps it won't be missed.

But over and above the hope and the fear about the new world is a third emotion that commentators have spotted in the transitional time, a feeling that will probably continue in the new world, and will have to be dealt with. That feeling is grief.

A TIME TO MOURN

There was a picture that was much reproduced in 2019, when the old, self-reliant world was at its most powerful. It showed the body of a man on the bank of the Rio Grande River. Next to his body was the body of his little girl. They had drowned together trying to reach safety in the United States, safety from violence and poverty in their home country. They did not reach the new world.

Every day now the news is full of people who won't be in the new world on the other side of the pandemic. More old than young, more black and brown than white, more poor and homeless and physically frail than prosperous and healthy, they died during the crossing.

No matter who or what makes it to the other side, there will be – there must be if that world is to be better than the one it is replacing – grief for our losses. Pope Francis at Easter reminded us of the medical people and the priests who died in Italy, especially in Bergamo, during the pandemic.

A little paradoxically, grief is also an important part of the new life after addiction, grief for what must be left behind. Bob Kocher, an organizer of travel events for recovering people, tells the moving story online of how he wept when he was newly sober when he realized that he was leaving behind what had seemed like his only real friends: alcohol and other drugs. He was leaving behind the person he had been for a long time. In time he grew to love his new, recovering self, but there had to be a moment when he felt stripped of everything he knew and trusted.

So I think we will have to grieve, not just the people whom the virus has claimed, but the people we ourselves used to be. Sure, we may have been insensitive to the misery of people around us, and blind to the environmental damage we were causing. We can become better people, and we have examples of that all around us during these hard times. But there was familiarity and ease in the people we used to be. In the last few years, in fact, we had gone to great lengths to surround ourselves with people like ourselves, and to distance ourselves from those from whom we differed. Now we will have to experience change; now we have become dependent on the kindness of strangers.

We might prefer to "light out for the territory," to run away, like that quintessential American, Huck Finn, or like Ammon Bundy. But as every Western story, movie, or TV show ever made announces, there is no "territory." The Frontier had closed by 1890. Instead, there is only the environment, and it is finite and limited. If we refuse to care for it thoughtfully, if we refuse to deal with it as communities, not as utterly autonomous individuals, it must resist us with the weapons at its disposal, like viruses.

As the many experts on grief tell us, it takes time and comes in stages or waves. I hope we will have the comfort of restored virtues like compassion and humor as we deal with our losses. But there will be moments when we will gasp with pain when we look back on the days before the pandemic, when we remember all that we took for granted, when we look at the gap where someone or something used to be.

Chapter 6

A Time Out

Something was said at an online meeting the other day that struck a lot of us forcefully: a participant opined that the pandemic was God's way of giving humanity a time-out. This analogy is rich in implication.

First, why did we need a time-out?

A more mature being gives a time-out to a less evolved being because the less evolved is throwing a tantrum, often involving harm to others and a decline in the local quality of life. There were a lot of tantrums being thrown in the world before the pandemic, a world that we seem luckily to be leaving behind. These tantrums occurred because a lot of people had been infected with the idea, adrift in the cultural air we all breathed, that finally the time had come for all of us to get our own way, dammit. Many people were quoting Howard Beale in *Network*, "I'm mad as hell and I'm not going to take it anymore!"

A lot of two-year-olds would say the same thing several times a day if they had the words for it. It may also be worth keeping in mind that Howard Beale is insane, and in the end dies by the violence he incites with his war-cry. He has lost his mind, in this forty-three-year-old movie, for a very topical reason: he is in later middle age, and he has lost his job. Underneath his contagious rage is the fear that he has become the hapless victim of time and economic change. He also drinks a little, if I recall; his closest professional friend is played by William Holden, who IRL eventually drank himself to death (i.e., fell while [typically] drunk, hit his head, bled to death). This kind of anger may be "the dubious luxury of normal men," but it is "poison" for alcoholics (BB, p. 66). So a time-out would be a better choice during angry times.

Second, what good do time-outs produce?

When two-year-olds are given a time-out, they get to go into a quieter environment, to be by themselves. During the time-out they are supposed to think about different, more socially positive choices. When enough time goes by for the two-year-old to be restored to sanity, to be ready to act upon those better choices, the time-out ends. In a similar way, the pandemic has given many of us the opportunity to stay home, using only our devices – many of which involve pauses before the "Send" command – for making our needs known. Perhaps we are becoming aware of better, more prosocial choices during this time-out.

What people on a time-out are doing, whatever their age, is contemplating change. Of course at first during the pandemic time-out we tried to stay busy, acting as if nothing very much was different. But after a few days we realized how silly that was: as we adapted each day to new, unimaginable restrictions, it dawned on all of us that we were well on our way to a new state of life. So a lot of people began using this hiatus to ask the sort of question that recovering people are urged to consider: not "How can I get other people to grant me my way?" but "How can I change so that I can be content no matter what other people do, no matter how things go?" A wise 12 Stepper was once asked, "How can I believe in a Higher Power when nothing goes my way?" He replied, "Don't have a way."

Naturally many other people have refused to get quiet and meditate.

Instead they are doing what a lot of un-recovering people do: they are stepping up their demands for their way. They are forming groups and marching, in defiance of their state governments, chanting "We want our way! We want our way!" As has been pointed out, forming groups and marching is a good way to be exposed to the virus. Tantrums are self- defeating.

The *12 X 12* long ago pointed out the fallacy of marching and chanting, at least for alcoholics. In the commentary on Step 2, the step about returning to sanity, these sentences appear, all on one page (31): "As psychiatrists have often observed, *defiance* is the outstanding characteristic of many an alcoholic. So it's not strange that lots of us have had our day *defying* God Himself. ... When we encountered a 12 Step program, the fallacy of our *defiance* was revealed. ... No man, we saw, could believe in God and *defy* Him, too. Belief meant reliance, not *defiance*." All the italics are mine, and I hope they make clear what the point is. To defy, like Howard Beale, is to stay stuck.

BEYOND DEFIANCE

For the lifesaving change that is recovery to take place, the alcoholic has to abandon denial for honesty, the one quality that the Big Book insists is essential for recovery. Alcoholics also have to replace defiance with – well, the suggested 12 Step quality is humility. The *Big Book* and the *12 X 12* try to define humility, especially apropos of Step 7 ("Humbly asked God to remove our shortcomings.") This literature delicately tries to describe this quality without setting off addicts, who are hypersensitive to perceived slights. But maybe we can settle for this simple idea: humility is the opposite of defiance. A watchword in Al-Anon is that it's a good idea to practice saying, "You may well be right."

The time-out given us by the pandemic might be a very good time to contemplate less defiance and more cooperation. Every day we hear and see stories about people confined to home learning how to get along and make things work there. It's worth recalling that the virus is really small: threatening it with a big weapon, like angry crowds, won't impress it.

Perhaps in the end this is what will signal that we can safely come out of our time-out: when we are ready to work together constructively with other grown-ups to care for the most vulnerable creatures, humans and beasts alike. The quarantine can end when a significant percentage of our species most readily says, not "I want my way!" but "How can I help?" This is the real "herd immunity" that people have begun to talk about: enough physically and morally healthy people that the virus of *defiance* can't get a foothold.

Chapter 7

❧

Martha Stewart and the Environment

I have spoken about the coronavirus as a message from the environment, but I don't want you to imagine The Environment as a T Rex from *Jurassic Park*, or as Godzilla, who was always a peevish voice against environmental depredation. Many of us meet The Environment in a far more amiable way, particularly on the Internet. We click on adorable pictures of cats and dogs; some of us, like me, are lucky enough to have actual pets. They live with us, because they and their forebears have crossed the line between humans and nature and have made a home there.

Please don't spread the word that I have a cat, a fact that only a few thousand people know. Strictly speaking, Jesuits aren't supposed to have pets. And indeed dogs in Jesuit communities can get pretty squirrelly (so to speak) by trying to become codependent with every one of the odd collection of personal traits presented by a group of

Jesuits of any size (say, more than two). Cats, luckily, are rarely eligible for Al-Anon, since they maintain healthy boundaries around themselves.

How did I get a cat? Lower companions, of course. Thirty years ago I lived in a Jesuit community in another state that had cats then, and has had them ever since. Then, twelve years ago, I was assigned to a parish that had two cats when I was assigned, and three when I arrived a few months later.

The alpha cat at this three-cat parish was named after the parish, St. Leo.

Leo the cat got his name because he showed up in the Emergency Services line one day. (St. Leo, like many Jesuit parishes, is in the inner city, and has always had a strong outreach to the marginal people in its neighborhood.) The line dwindled until finally there was just one homeless guy and an unnamed young cat. After the guy was helped and was leaving, the parishioner who had met his need reminded him to take his cat. He replied, like the concierge did to Inspector Clouseau, "But that is not my cat." So the cat was adopted by, and named after, the parish. Since a parish staffer who was in charge of the food pantry was allergic, Leo ended up in the parish parsonage, not the offices.

The years went by, and two other cats and I both came to dwell in the parsonage. One day Leo, usually a saturnine and stealthy fellow, ran to the front window and became uncharacteristically demonstrative. A female cat from the streets had come up on the parsonage porch, and Leo, despite having been fixed, was welcoming her gallantly. This happened more than once, so I named the street cat Leontyne. This has nothing to do with the great American soprano Leontyne Price, whom, like most sensible people, I adore. It was a back-formation from Leo, and so another tribute to a wonderfully generous parish.

More years went by. Leontyne would come by for a while, and then disappear for a season. She was always

very timid; even though we would put food out on the
porch for her, she ran away if the pastor or I came near
her. Until one day ... Leontyne didn't run; she sat at our
door mewling pitiably. She was sick, emaciated, pregnant
(it turned out), with dirty, matted fur. She was saying as
clearly as she could that she wanted to come in out of the
cold. (It was May, but it can stay cold and wet in the
Northwest until the 4th of July.)

After a day or two, the pastor and I decided to take
Leontyne in. Our vet, who is a St. Leo's parishioner, had
warned that the fourth cat makes you a Cat Lady, but Fr.
Steve and I reasoned that we would say that we had two
cats apiece to avoid criticism. So we took in Leontyne and
nursed her back to health. Her kittens were too frail to
survive, but with regular food, warmth and light, and
regular brushing, she turned out to be an elegant house
cat, with the face of a Maine Coon and the body of – well,
not a Venus, but a much smaller frame than Maine Coons
usually have. And whiskers galore.

More years have gone by, and I still have her. She is
still timid with most other people, but she completely
trusts me, in no small part because of Martha Stewart.
When my cat and I were still getting acquainted, I bought a
Martha Stewart cat brush – luckily; for some reason Ms.
Stewart was only invested in pet products for a brief
period. To this day, Leontyne thinks that brush is among
humanity's finest achievements, like the Mona Lisa or the
Panama Canal.

In a sense Leontyne was socially distancing long
before it was fashionable. Two of the three cats who got to
the parsonage before her were male, Leo and big, dumb,
sweet Toby, and she got along fine with them. However the
other cat was Samantha, a Russian Blue countess who slept
curled up in the pastor's left armpit. All the other cats
outweighed Samantha, Toby by quite a lot, but Samantha
nevertheless ruled with an iron paw. It was hate at first
sight between her and Leontyne. From the beginning,

Samantha would patrol outside my room and pounce on Leontyne if she poked her nose out. This was sad for Leontyne, but it meant that she and I became very good friends, as I brushed her whenever I wasn't working at church. A few years later I moved to a different Jesuit community in Tacoma, but in our second Jesuit home, some were allergic to cats, so Leontyne has stayed in my room all the years I've had her.

And oh she's been a boon during the pandemic. When I'm scared because I'm old and alcoholic and easily depressed, or when I can't put up for another minute with those odd traits of Jesuits that I mentioned before, Leontyne rolls over on her back on the heating pad that used to be mine, and I get the Martha Stewart brush, and I know that I am making one creature perfectly happy. Of course since I am now home all the time, the old arrangement where there were special brushing times before and after parish hours has gone by the boards. The rule now is that, unless she's asleep or eating, brushing is a strong possibility.

I send pictures of her by phone and email to loved ones, including Annie L., and I know the pictures help them to regain their equilibrium, so easily lost these days. And my loved ones send me pictures of puppies and kittens, dogs and cats. For blessedly, I am bi – I love cats and dogs.

Chapter 8

A Bridge Too Far

S ome friends have told me about an emotional moment they have experienced during the pandemic. Suddenly they were overcome with a sense of loss, as if someone they loved had died, even though that had not happened – and though many people are experiencing grief for loved ones who have died of the virus. In time I had such a moment myself.

GRIEF AND THE PANDEMIC

It came, curiously enough, after I wrote the section on grief a few chapters back. While I was writing, I was describing what my friends had told me, and noting that grief seemed like an appropriate reaction to all the changes and losses that the pandemic was bringing. People have referred to Elizabeth Kubler-Ross's phases of grief, and noted that the final stage is "acceptance," an important concept in 12 Step recovery. The Serenity Prayer begins with "grant me the serenity to accept the things I cannot change." I would add that Kubler-Ross took pains to correct the notion that "acceptance" is necessarily a warm, positive feeling; instead it is the feeling one reaches when one is ready to face the hard facts without denial or minimizing. It's like the "honesty" that Chapter 5 of the *Big Book* says is essential for recovery.

But then I finished writing that passage, and went for a walk. In Tacoma we were finally having mild, sunny days after a long, cold, mostly dry winter. And I had been feeling a lot of cabin fever. Yet as I walked down the hill to a local nature preserve, I felt the crushing sadness that my friends had told me about. As with them, it wasn't spurred by news of deaths of people close to me – that hasn't happened. But wherever it came from, the sadness quickly got connected to all the losses I have sustained during my life.

Some of the hardest losses are those that Al-Anon deals with so skillfully. Alcoholism, and other chronic ills like mental illness, corrode the fiber of families. We hear that addiction, depression, mental illness, and domestic violence are all increasing during the lockdown, and many relationships, including families, will not survive to the World After. It is hard to grieve the loss of someone who has died; but at times it seems just as hard to miss someone who is still alive and lives not very far away, someone whose contact information one has or can readily get on the Internet. And yet there can be no contact, as surely as if an injunction were in place. And now, here it is, an illness that may end the lives of us who are older: will the no-contact rule outlive us? Will we never see these living loved ones again?

FAITH AND THE BRIDGE

It took me some time, some reaching out to supportive friends, to get past this moment, when it was hard for me to care what the post-pandemic world would look like. Some recovering people would say that what is needed at such a moment of dark discouragement is a boost of faith or hope, along the lines of Step 2: "Came to believe that a Power greater than ourselves could restore us to Sanity."

This Step is addressed in Chapter 4 of the *Big Book*, "We Agnostics," the chapter before the Steps. Chapter 4 addresses the concerns of those who feel like they can't muster even the minimal faith in some sort of Higher Power that Steps like 2 suggest. Bill Wilson, who had a weakness for elaborate metaphors, talks about that last step toward faith, Step 2, in this way: "Some of us had already walked far over the Bridge of Reason toward the desired shore of faith. The outlines and the promise of the New Land had brought luster to tired eyes and fresh courage to flagging spirits. Friendly hands had stretched out in welcome. We were grateful that Reason had brought us so far. But somehow, we couldn't quite step ashore. Perhaps we had been leaning too heavily on Reason that last mile and we did not like to lose our support" (53).

We can use "Reason" to try to imagine "the New Land" on the other side of the chasm of the pandemic. But in the end, as Bill says, something more than Reason has to close the gap. It's rather like that moment in the third Indiana Jones movie, when Jones has to step out over a deep canyon to save his father's life. When he does so, as he does so, he realizes that there is a bridge over the gap, invisible until you've stepped on to it because it's camouflaged to look like the bottom of the canyon.

THROWING THE BRIDGE

Or consider this if, like me, you've run out of bridge, and lost hope that there is a New Land beyond, or that you will get across the chasm. The year I got sober, an American novelist, Mark Helprin, published a long, strange novel called *Winter's Tale*. It is set in New York City, where the pandemic of 2020 has now caused great loss, but it is not the New York City of common life. Part of the story of *Winter's Tale* involves time travel, and this is one of the more ordinary features of life in this novel.

We need not concern ourselves with the elaborate plot of the novel. I'm citing it only for one reason: one plot-strand involves the building of a bridge from Manhattan to one of the other boroughs. In the background here is the Brooklyn Bridge, which long since achieved mythic status in American culture, even before Hart Crane consecrated it in his epic *The Bridge*. The bridge under construction in *Winter's Tale* somehow crosses, not just space, but time. It represents a concentrated effort by the human spirit to create something beyond us, something like the cure for the coronavirus that is being feverishly sought all over the world.

The principal reason I'm thinking of Helprin during the pandemic is because of one element from the lore of bridge-building that he provides his readers. He says – and I assume he didn't invent this – that the engineers and all the workers who risk their lives to construct a bridge say, not that they are "building" a bridge, but that they are "throwing" it. Just like the alcoholic at the edge of the Bridge of Reason, bridge-builders "throw" the bridge into space and time, trusting that beyond their blueprints and caissons, the span will land on the other side. It takes enormous courage and sacrifice. Three men died in the digging of the pylons for the Brooklyn Bridge because its builders didn't know about the "bends," the sometimes fatal effects of sudden huge changes in atmospheric pressure. At least twenty-four others died from falls and other accidents.

Once again, recovering people may be at an advantage in these hard times. We know what it's like to "throw" a bridge, the bridge of recovery, a guess, a hunch, a starveling hope that we can reach a New Land, a land where we can become New People. And in the face of the fear and despair, now is the time to "throw" a bridge across the pandemic, to believe and hope that there is a New Land where people lay down their lives to help other people find healing and a second chance. Desperation and cynicism must not have the last word: we are seeing people every day who are better than that.

Chapter 9

❧

Turn on the Lights for G's Nona

I n a couple of weeks, if I don't take a drink, I'll have another sobriety anniversary: the actual date is May 7. I mention that because already on that first alcohol-free May 7th I was worried to death about how I was going to get through the Christmas holidays without drinking. Since then I have noticed that everybody who stops drinking, at any time of the year, shares the same fear.

THE PANDEMIC AND THE PINK CLOUD

I don't think this is just another example of distorted alcoholic thinking. I believe that something similar occurs for everyone who is undergoing a change of heart, what in the Gospels is called a *metanoia*. The fear that arises in short order is that it won't be possible to sustain those changes "for the rest of my life." C. S. Lewis notes in *The Screwtape Letters* that new religious converts struggle with this fear. Worrying about abstinent holidays is just a specifically alcoholic form of it.

We seem to have reached a similar point in the way people are reacting to the pandemic. There were so many uplifting stories of creative generosity in the first few weeks of the quarantine. One from my home state of Washington went viral. In Vancouver (no, not the one in Canada) there was a check-out man in a grocery store. He was deaf, but adept at reading lips. Then customers began to wear face masks, and he could no longer discern what they wanted, and he feared for his job.

In the brutal old days before the pandemic hit, perhaps outraged customers would have complained on Facebook about his poor service, and he would have been fired. But in the face of the pandemic, his co-workers came to his aid: they put up signs at his checkout stand explaining the situation to customers; they gave him a tear-off pad where customers could write what they wanted him to understand. The customers were more than happy to help; some wrote him appreciative notes for working at this risky time. He was deeply grateful to his work colleagues.

Now a few more weeks of the pandemic have gone by, and other, less edifying stories are appearing. In some states protesters have marched on behalf of ending social distancing, and beaches have been opened. The pseudo-Darwinian idea that we should sacrifice some less productive members of our society, who "were on their last legs, anyway," has gotten a hearing.

This is not just compassion fatigue, of course. Many people were living from paycheck to paycheck before the pandemic hit, and they are desperate to feed themselves and their families. The Seattle-Tacoma area has some of the highest rental rates in the country, and a modest check from the government simply won't go very far around here to secure housing. At this date there are ominous rumblings about a second wave of the virus next fall, with much worse medical and economic effects. So compassion and joy are giving way to grasping fear.

Often in early recovery there is a similar period of euphoria during which other people, life, and we ourselves suddenly look more hopeful than they have in years. It's such a powerful lift that it's easy to wonder if we have entered an alternate reality, a computer simulation, a cheery Twilight Zone where all our dreams come true. Recovering people call this the "pink cloud" phase.

After any conversion, there is in time a loss of optimism: the "pink cloud" abruptly ends. What can we do when the dark facts of human fear return, as they have now in this phase of the pandemic? The Steps and the people at the meetings are an invaluable help at getting through this psychological dip: sagging newcomers are advised to work "the Program." The Program, which is pretty much the Steps, urges the alcoholic to find a new, solid foundation.

WORKING THE STEPS AND GROWING UP

Another word for this solid foundation is maturity. Steps 4 through 9 especially are about meeting one's commitments, being a mensch. If you broke it, admit it and offer to fix it, "it" being any professional or personal relationship you have formed and damaged. Once you have worked Steps 4-9, and then incorporate those Steps in your daily life with 10 and 11, in 12 you get down to "principles," solid rock on which you can build a life. You have finally become a grown-up.

It's a great help at this turning point to be surrounded by people who have taken the Steps and are living the kind of compassionate and courageous lives that millions of people are these days – medical and emergency workers, grocery employees, including the friends of the man who reads lips. Sure, there are people who make poorer choices these days, not just the people who are willing to risk other people's lives, but also the con artists, including some preachers, who are trying to cash in on the pandemic with various bogus fixes. But we need to focus on people who are making a moral success of their lives, many of whom are risking their own lives and the lives of their families. I know some personally, whose stories I could tell; so do you, and you should attend to them to keep your hope, and your sanity, alive.

LIGHTS ON FOR THE FUTURE

Last Friday we Washingtonians did something beautiful. At 8:20 p.m. – 20:20 in military parlance – high schools around the state turned on their stadium lights. Seniors in the Class of 2020 who have had to forego prom and graduation ceremonies drove around the stadium, with or without parents and siblings, and honked and flashed their lights. I live at a Jesuit high school, Bellarmine, in Tacoma: the members of the Jesuit community went over to the stadium and waved and yelled while the kids drove by. We had taped up little signs to let the grads know our love and support.

I don't know who came up with the idea, but I loved it. One of the cars that I was especially watching out for contained not just a grad, but his grandmother, who's a great pal of mine from the parish where I work. She's a well-known figure around Bellarmine. When her grandson, "G," was announced as prom royalty last fall, she put his sash on at half-time of the homecoming game. Since she is Italian, everybody knows her as his "nona," so that was the cheer that went up last fall – "G's Nona! "G's Nona!" I made sure that "Nona" and her grandson knew I was there when they went by last Friday.

So my advice, even as things seem darker on some days of the pandemic, is, turn on the lights and cheer. And I give this advice first to myself, because we're all scared together. Recovering people say that the Higher Power wouldn't have brought us this far only to drop us now. When I was drinking, I couldn't imagine a life after stopping – but there is one. I remember that now on days when I can't imagine a life after the pandemic.

Chapter 10

ৼ৶৹

Relying on God

W hat's starting to wear on me more than the daily mix of fear and boredom is uncertainty about the future, even though I try to focus on One Day at a Time.

GOD'S WILL, STEP 3, AND STEP 11

The more sensible voices at this point are saying that there will be a brief lull in the pandemic during the summer of 2020, at least in the Northern Hemisphere. But they also maintain that it will come back in the fall in a "second wave." They say that discovery and distribution of an effective vaccine won't happen until well after that. So presumably in September or October we may go back into quarantine, perhaps for much longer than our current restrictions. What the economic, much less the psychological, effects of this will be are too frightening to dwell on, at least for me.

The Steps I try to focus on when anxiety comes are 3 and 11. I've noticed something about these Steps: some people say that the difficulty with Step 3 – "Made a decision to turn our will and our lives over to the care of God as we understood Him" – is that it is hard to know and to act on the will of God. But strictly speaking Step 3 isn't about God's will; the only "will" it mentions is mine. Of course it is plenty difficult to know my will – the real one underneath the rationalizations – so this doesn't make the Step a snap. But the aspect of God that it does mention is God's "care," and that's a comfort. We may struggle to know God's will, but we can be certain of God's care amid our struggles.

I think God's care sustains us in the Steps between 3 and 11. As we try to know ourselves and to use that knowledge to heal broken relationships (Steps 4-5, 8-9), we continue to rely on God's care. We renew our trust in that care in Steps 6 and 7, where we ask God to fix us, knowing that we can no more fix ourselves by ourselves than we could stop drinking. God's will does eventually show up, but only in Step 11: "Sought through prayer and meditation to improve our conscious contact with God as we understood Him, praying only for knowledge of His will for us and the power to carry that out." When we first turn our will and our lives over to God, we only know that God cares; what God will want us to do in our turn we couldn't bear to learn until we had taken the intervening Steps. In those Steps we face the anger and the fear that have blocked us from knowing and doing God's will, the anger and fear that we have drowned out with our addiction.

People sometimes ask if one can or should take Step 3 just once or repeatedly. Answers differ, but the one that is truest to my experience appears in a quotation from C. S. Lewis that my friend Tom Weston, S.J., has called to our attention: "Relying on God has to begin all over again every day as if nothing had yet been done." The only change in my working of Step 3 over the years has been that I now have a big chunk of time in which I have tried to trust God, and a set of results produced by that trust.

But every day when the question arises, "Will I trust God today – now in the middle of a pandemic, with a gloomy forecast – since I've gotten pretty good results for many years by doing so? Or will I go back to my old ideas and do it my way, the way that produced such dismal results for the first thirty-seven years of my life?" The best I can manage in response is the old Jack Benny punchline, "I'm thinking, I'm thinking!"

(For anyone too young to remember Jack Benny: his schtick was that he – or his comic persona – was incredibly cheap; when a mugger jumps him in a dark alley and utters the classic line "Your money or your life," Jack answers as above.)

Some days are a little better than others. Some days I feel like I've been skillfully steered to help somebody in a way that feels way beyond my insights or abilities, and then I can move to trust more quickly. But these days I don't interact much with people, so on a lot of days it's hard work to decide to trust. And of course I trust only for this day; I hold with Lewis that tomorrow I'll have to do it all again.

THOMAS MERTON AND STEP 3

Still it's a help that I've landed on trust for many days, at least on enough trust that I've relied on God rather than alcohol to get me through the dark nights. And it helps that, largely through the practice of the Steps, I think I know more about myself and about God than I did when I started.

There's a wonderful prayer on this subject of self-knowledge and God's will that I didn't think much of when I first read it as a young man. It's by Thomas Merton, who did a lot of growing during his years as a Trappist monk: "Dear God, I have no idea where I am going. I do not see the road ahead of me. I cannot know for certain where it will end. Nor do I really know myself, and the fact that I think that I am following Your will does not mean that I am actually doing so. But I believe this: I believe that the desire to please You does in fact please You. I hope I have that desire in everything I do. I hope I never do anything apart from that desire. And I know that if I do this You will lead me by the right road though I may know nothing about it at the time. Therefore I will trust You always for though I may seem to be lost and in the shadow of death I will not be afraid because I know You will never leave me to face my troubles all alone."

I first saw Merton's prayer when I was in the Jesuit novitiate, which I began just shy of 18. I thought it was a poor excuse for a prayer. Shouldn't a monk who had so much time at his disposal know all about himself?

Shouldn't he have planned out his future, including some detours, like a grown-up should? How could he not know where he was going? I did. Why tie yourself in spiritual knots about knowing the will of God? Isn't God's will obvious to any sensible person?

Merton's prayer looked a lot different to me after the years went by.

Being alcoholic had not been part of my life plan. Indeed, I thought becoming a Jesuit would guarantee that I could leave such sordid matters behind me. When alcoholism happened in me, I had no plan at all for dealing with it. Lacking a plan, I desperately did what a bunch of drunks told me to do, even though none of them had the kind of prestigious doctorate that I had drunk my way to. And I got better, and life got better, even though I didn't "know [any]thing about it at the time."

So here we are, in the middle of a deadly disease outbreak. On any day, it's easy to feel "lost and in the shadow of death." What is helping us is knowing, through Zoom meetings and other interchanges, that we do not have "to face [our] troubles all alone." I haven't kept track of how many days we have been sheltering at home, but however many it's been, so far I've been able each day to trust in God's will. Tomorrow? Well . . .

Chapter 11

❧ ❧

Our Daily Blog

S ome states are beginning in small ways to lift the ban on people gathering. This only makes folks like me more impatient for the quarantine to end. I was talking on the phone to parishioners this morning, and we were already making plans for the first Mass after we can all get back together in some form.

But a running theme in all I have written is that we'll have to get through this One Day at a Time. Whatever the post-pandemic world will bring, good or bad, isn't here today. I emailed my family yesterday that my big thrill last week was going out to Walgreen's and getting my routine prescriptions through the drive-through lane: that was the task of that day.

OUR DAILY(?) BREAD

This spiritual principle is contained in the central Christian prayer, simply called "The Lord's [i.e., Jesus's] Prayer." It begins "Our Father." It falls into two halves: In the first God is praised and asked to accomplish great things; in the second, God is asked to do the humble things that human beings need within God's will. The words at the pivot from Part 1 to Part 2 are "Give us this day our daily bread." We ask God to meet our needs one day at a time.

It's a very familiar prayer to most people, but there is a real mystery about one of the central words in the Greek text of it in the Gospel of Matthew. But before we take that up, note that the prayer that we say is included in the Sermon on the Mount in Matthew's Gospel. However, it also turns up in the Gospel of Luke – but there it's much shorter. Scholars believe that the Luke version is older, because we can imagine somebody adding to it sooner than somebody dropping parts of it. But both versions contain the same mystifying word.

It's the word translated "daily." In Greek it's *epiousios*. Greek builds up words by putting together words that are separate parts of speech in English, and so here. The roots for *epiousios* are two very common words in Greek. *Epi* is a preposition that means "upon, on," or "for," "for the purpose of." *Ousios* is ultimately from the most fundamental verb in Greek, or in fact in most languages, the verb "to be." So judging from the roots, *epiousios* would seem to mean "for being," or "for existing."

The problem is that, so far as we know, this word was only used twice in any Greek documents that we have: in the Gospel of Matthew and in the Gospel of Luke. So we have no other uses of it to guide us to its exact meaning. It's unique (the technical term is *hapax legomenon*, "read only once").

From early on, this led students of the Gospels to wonder exactly what this word, and this verse, means. There has been a great deal of discussion. To keep it simple, it probably does mean something like "for each day," or "for keeping us going day by day." But it has strange overtones, and theologians have often wondered if it has a larger meaning: that is, is "bread" a metaphor for everything we need to get through each day, and is *epiousios* then a hint that what we need, we need very badly – it's a matter of life and death for God to give us what we need, we can't keep going without it. In the Latin translation of Matthew's Gospel, made some 400 years after the Greek text, it became *supersubstantialem*, "above substance," and with that theologians were off to the races with metaphysical notions.

But let's stick to the original Greek text, and agree that the prayer is asking for all the things we need to survive today. The pandemic has greatly sharpened our awareness of these, and of how many people are deprived of them. We need air, light, clean water, food, clothing, shelter, companionship (by the way, a "companion" is literally someone you break bread with). To lack these – and the virus kills by riding on moisture in air and impeding our ability to breathe – is dangerous and can be fatal. There is growing concern about the food supply, even in a well-fed country like the United States.

Farmers are throwing away foodstuffs for lack of a market; people line up for miles to get food.

OUR DAILY REPRIEVE

For 12 Steppers, "daily bread" can easily be taken as a symbol for the daily grace to stay in recovery. For substance abusers, it's about the grace not to use our substance today, but beyond that the ability to abstain precisely with grace, without being emotionally brittle. So fundamental is this for recovering people that we have become converts to programs like Zoom in the hundreds of thousands since the pandemic began: online meetings are where we get our "daily bread." The "bread" we find there is in the form of the stories that are told, but also of the faces of the storytellers. As I've fumbled with the technology involved, sometimes I've only had the audio, sometimes only the video, but for real nourishment I think we need both.

"Daily" also has the ring of humility: we aren't asking for anything grandiose or highfalutin, just what anybody has to have to make it to tomorrow. Smartphones make it possible to see and hear, but they capture our likenesses in un-retouched close-ups. Zoom portraits are as merciless as passport photos or drivers' licenses. But then the whole purpose of the Steps is to get down to who we really are, because it's only from that place that we can honestly ask God for the most basic things we need. We don't need Botox; we need our daily bread.

One more implication of "daily" for me is coming up in what you are reading. When I sat down to write all the books I've put out so far – the ones that were published and the many more that weren't – I already had a pretty good idea of how their parts would go together. But for this book, Annie's book, it's been a very different process. I had some ideas when I started, but it soon morphed into whatever was on my mind that day. At most I might jot down a few thoughts at the end of a particular section about what might come next. All through I have been asking of God, "Give us this day our daily chapter," or "our daily blog," except I'm not blogging.

All I can tell you is that, One Day at a Time, God has been faithful.

And I just thought of what I might write about tomorrow.

Chapter 12

≈⇁

Faithful God

I told this story before, in *A 12 Step Approach to the Sunday Readings*. I began my Jesuit life at the Jesuit novitiate in Florissant, a northern suburb of St. Louis, where I had grown up. It wasn't that far from where Lewis and Clark set off to explore the American Northwest, where I eventually ended up.

THE WRITING ON THE NOVITIATE WALL

In the novitiate was a large classroom, on the second floor. This was where the Master of Novices, Fr. Charlie Hunter, S. J., taught us, most days, about prayer. I would of course never have called him "Charlie." Even when I met him again, 30 years later when I was a priest, a college teacher, and a full-fledged Jesuit myself, I still called him "Father." He was an interesting guy: he was from Belize, a formerly British colony in the Caribbean. Belize, known for its first 150 years as British Honduras, was the product of a double revolt, not just against Spain, like all its Central American neighbors, but then against those neighbors as well: the revolt was engineered by an unlikely coalition of white British colonists, their black slaves, and an indigenous Caribbean people, the Garifuna. Fr. Hunter combined these strains: though born in Belize to an old family, he had been educated in England in the Latin classics. When he was my novice master, he was veddy British, loved Cardinal Newman, and blessedly told us that the most important value in the spiritual life was – no, not being right or doing right – courtesy. He quoted Belloc and Chesterton on this subject.

Over the door of the classroom where Fr. Hunter tried to turn us into Victorian gentlemen a motto was painted in flowing script. It was a quotation from Paul's *First Letter to the Corinthians* (1:9). Of course it was in Latin; in 1963, before Vatican II changed so much, everything was in Latin. It read: *Fidelis Deus: per quem vocati estis in Societate filii ejus Jesu Christi Domini nostri*. After four years of Latin in high school, and a prize or two, I had no trouble understanding it: "God [is] faithful: [it is] through God that you have been called into the society of God's son, Jesus Christ our Lord."

There was a play on words in *Societate*, "society": Paul meant the community – *koinonia* in his Greek—of the early Christian church, specifically the infant church community in the busy Greek seaport of Corinth. But "Society of Jesus" is also the official name of the Jesuits in Latin (in Spanish it's the *Compania de Jesus*, "The Companions of Jesus").

Several times a day we went into that room, under that legend, to pray or to listen to Fr. Hunter. And just about every time those words comforted me. At that time the reassurance I needed was that it hadn't been a terrible mistake my entering the Society of Jesus. Only much later would it have occurred to me that *I* might have made the mistake; back then I worried that the Society of Jesus had made the mistake in accepting me. My signing up had happened rather suddenly, when Pope John XXIII died the day after I graduated from the Jesuit high school in St. Louis. And there had been a lot of misgivings on their part.

FAITHFUL THROUGH THE YEARS

So I needed the comfort of that verse. It helped to know that God was faithful. It was a relief when I could believe, at least intermittently, that my being a Jesuit wasn't some twisted notion of mine, but was actually an idea, however implausible, of God's. I hadn't been the pious type during my Jesuit high school years. As anyone around at the time would still testify, I was instead the smart-ass type. That line of Latin continued to be a comfort over the years, when more and more of my contemporaries decided that in fact they had *not* been called into the Society, and left.

I needed that comfort even more twenty years later, when I had become a "first class alcoholic prospect." When I was in treatment, at a secular rehab – not specifically for priests – I was pretty sure that, whatever the result of treatment would be in terms of my drinking, the most likely outcome was that the Jesuits and I would agree, as amicably as we could, that my being a Jesuit had all been a horrible mistake. And I would now slip out the door quietly.

That isn't what happened. God *is* faithful, in ways that I couldn't imagine or aspire to then. It turned out that being in recovery was a very good way for me to be a Jesuit. All along God was being crafty. All along I was being called. Because of the support I'm getting these days on Zoom from many companions, men and women in recovery, I suspect I'm actually doing better psychologically during the quarantine than some of the Jesuits I live with. As I said in Chapter 11, I have a practice of learning to trust God all over each day. I don't count how many days it's been since we locked down; I don't (mostly) try to guess how many more days this will continue.

Being "called" is an experience that a lot of recovering people get to have. They call it "working the 12th Step." Whenever they carry the message of 12 Step recovery to somebody, whether that person is brand new or has been in recovery thirty years, they get to feel that they are the right person in the right place at the right time. They get to feel that a reliable Higher Power has chosen them for a job they are uniquely qualified to perform, not in spite of, but because of, some seriously awkward life experiences.

When I met Fr. Hunter again, thirty years after the novitiate, we had both been through some changes. After many years in the United States as a professor of Classics and as Master of Novices, he returned to Belize in his late fifties. There he transformed into a firebrand of Caribbean literary and cultural consciousness. He went from being Winston Churchill to Bob Marley. When we met again, I was with a student group from Seattle University on a Third World experience in Belize. As I mentioned, I did not try to be chummy with Fr. Hunter. For one thing, I was too grateful for his lessons in courtesy to be rude – courtesy, I had learned from him, will take you far in life and especially in ministry. But I did ask him about Caribbean literature: I asked him about the Nobel prize winning Caribbean poet Derek Walcott. He told me which poems to start with – shorter, easier poems, not Walcott's great Caribbean version of the Odyssey.

Then, as so often, I went a little too far. During those thirty years I had done a thing or two myself. I was eleven years sober, for one thing. But more to the point, I had a doctorate in Victorian literature. However, when I tried to suggest that perhaps this entitled me to consider myself something like Fr. Hunter's colleague, he got very uncomfortable with me. That's OK. The same God called both of us, and I didn't need to have Fr. Hunter tell me I had turned out all right. He died a year or two later, and I'm glad that we had our little moment when we could courteously disregard the fact that I had tried to rise above my station in life, like a footman at Downton Abbey.

Chapter 13

❧

Getting Even

Back when I was new in recovery, there was, in a Denver suburb, an old-timer named Don. He had something like twenty-seven years of sobriety, which seemed stratospheric to me then. When Don spoke, he liked to end with this: he thought it was important for him to "get even" with people – not for the wrongs they had done him, but for the good things. He did this by in his turn doing good things for others, and he urged his listeners to do the same.

I think Don was suggesting something that follows naturally from Steps 8 and 9: "Made a list of all people we had harmed, and became willing to make amends to them all," and "Made direct amends to such people wherever possible, except when to do so would injure them or others." "Getting even" is a neat summary of the effect of these Steps. If we act meanly or selfishly in a relationship, the relationship becomes uneven, unfair: One party is taking advantage of the other. In offering to "amend" the relationship, we are promising to make it "even," balancing give and take between the parties.

But Don's watchword also adds a nuance to these Steps. Instead of just talking about ceasing to harm and compensating for past harms, Don suggests that we practice gratitude and good acting as a response to the kindness that other people have shown us. I don't know whether I heard this or read this or thought it up, but I believe that it is possible at any given moment to feel gratitude or resentment – and gratitude is better.

One of the best things to come out of the pandemic is an outpouring of "getting even" with people who used to be ignored or even treated rudely. Television is suddenly flooded with pictures and sounds of people clapping, singing, cheering, for ordinary workers, not just medical workers, but grocery employees, car mechanics, truck drivers, factory workers who make face masks. Now that we have started "getting even," we realize that the list is endless. Imagine a new, post-pandemic society that is founded not on cutthroat competition, but on gratitude, on getting even.

AN ECONOMY BASED ON GIFTS

Actually someone long ago depicted such a society. I would like here to "get even" with a dear friend, the Rev. Carol Ludden. Carol was one of the first women to be ordained a priest in the Episcopal church. We were close friends for many years, and she taught me, as well as many other men and women, how to be a genuine pastor. She died after living for ten years with a form of cancer that she was told would kill her in four.

Carol turned me on to a remarkable book of spiritual reflection: *The Gift*, by Lewis Hyde. The only way to "get even" with all the riches of Hyde's book is to read it slowly and thoughtfully, so here I can only hint at his wealth of insights. Hyde was trying to study societies, like the Native peoples of the Pacific Northwest, in which success was measured, not by how much one had, as in capitalism, but by how much one gave away. He studied the Native institution of the "potlatch," in which a host did just that, gained prestige by how much he gave away. Hyde also studied many other societies, actual or proposed, which were founded in "the gift," in "getting even."

Of course 12 Step fellowships are just such a society. The 12th Step itself suggests that what a person should do with their recovery is to give it away completely by "carry[ing] the message to alcoholics." The official AA biography of Bill Wilson, its co-founder, is called *Pass It On*; this refers to a story in which a sober woman asks Bill how she can ever "get even" with him for the gift of AA, and he replies with the title of the book.

It will take a while for us to get past the pandemic, but the way – maybe the only way – to keep it from having the last word is to "get even" with it: to discern what gifts it may bring us. To remember gratitude as we are doing, and to re-found our nation on gratitude, would be a really extraordinary benefit. The watchword of Hugh, another recovering person in Denver back then, was "I forget to be grateful," his way of reminding himself to "get even."

I GET EVEN WITH FATHER SHEAHAN

You could call this "getting even" a "positive amends" if you needed a phrase for it. I made a very important "positive amend" in the course of my recovery. There was a wonderful Jesuit named Gerry Sheahan with whom I needed to "get even." Gerry was the principal of the Jesuit high school I attended: he made it financially possible when I cold-called him and told him that my family couldn't afford the tuition. He didn't ask me why; I'm not sure I would have or could have told him about the addictions that made my family bleed money.

So I went to that high school for four years, and then rather suddenly decided, the week after I graduated, that I wanted to "get even" with the Jesuits for my education by becoming one of them. As I mentioned earlier, not a few Jesuits were unenthusiastic about my wish. I'll never know the details, but I suspect Gerry supported my entry. He had my back, then and for many years later as I struggled, first with growing up, and later with getting sober (mind you these go hand in hand). He went from being principal of my high school to regional superior ("Provincial") and eventually to "American Assistant" – i.e., top Jesuit from the United States advising the Jesuit superior general in Rome. I don't know how many times he had to speak up for me when most other Jesuits were thoroughly tired of me.

When I had been sober something like fifteen years, I remembered what Denver Don said. So I wrote Gerry. By then I had moved to another "province" in another part of the country; I was teaching addictions counseling at a Jesuit university, and had written a book about weaving together the 12 Steps and Jesuit concepts. What I wrote to Gerry was that I was grateful for all he had done, and that I probably didn't know the half of it; and I also assured him that, on balance, he could feel like he hadn't backed a loser. He wrote a lovely note back. I saw him in person at a Jesuit conference a few months later; he was frail, but without using many words I thanked him again. The next year he died.

But not before I "got even."

Chapter 14

❧❧

The Life You Save
May Be Your Own

As I mentioned, one welcome feature of the pandemic world is the surge in gratitude to the many people who are saving lives at the risk of their own. There are many salutes to first responders, but also to people who save lives in less dramatic ways – by growing, harvesting, processing, and selling food, by keeping transportation and shipping going, by helping people to communicate with one another when it's not possible to do so in person.

I'm glad that we are noticing how many of these people there are, people whom a few weeks ago we paid little attention to, much less thanked. Spiritual growth is usually a matter of noticing more and noticing it more gratefully.

THE 12TH STEP SAVES LIVES

A story that is being covered in the news is the expected increase in mental health and addiction problems that is accompanying the spread of the virus. Some stories point out that, before the coronavirus, there was already a deadly epidemic in some of our poorer (and richer) communities – the spread of increasingly lethal opioids. Rock stars and athletes have moved on from commonplace painkillers and sedatives to exotic drugs used as surgical anesthetics, like fentanyl. The coronavirus is minimized in some quarters because it is especially deadly in the old and weak, as if such deaths were unimportant. But addictions are more likely to kill young people. Sometimes grieving families will never know whether a young person's overdose was an accident or suicide or a mix.

And in between the young and the old there is a new class of mortality in the United States, what are called "deaths of despair," especially among middle-aged men.

This might also be a time when 12 Step people can be reminded that they too save lives day after day.

Many people and billions of dollars are being devoted to finding some kind of medical solution to the pandemic. Meanwhile, 12 Step people have had a treatment for this older epidemic of drug addiction for eighty-five years. Astonishingly, it costs practically nothing in its pure, 12 Step form.

Twelve Step recovery begins with an acknowledgement of lack of power.

But the process leads practitioners to a place where they have the remarkable power to help other addicts simply by telling them their story. We hear a lot these days about "herd immunity" as a solution to the pandemic. By participating in a 12 Step fellowship, people can become members of a "herd" that remains "immune" to the deadly effects of the addiction, on the simple proviso of not "reinfecting" themselves by going back to the use of their substance or behavior of choice.

This is clear for people who are recovering from the abuse of substances, but there are also lifesavers among those who share healing with family members and friends affected by someone else's addiction. I have always believed that my mother might not have died at fifty-six if she had found Al-Anon some years earlier. She would have had much less stress, and more support for seeking the medical help that might have prevented her slow decline. We don't know exactly what killed her, but her life had worn her out at an age when many people these days are thriving and excited about new experiences.

I feel that my own life was saved by someone's intervention. I have expressed my gratitude to him many times over the years, in private and in public. The more I have reflected on what he did and how it changed my life, the more I owe him. And many people can and do save lives the same way.

SOMEONE SAVED MY LIFE TONIGHT

I need to be a little vague here. People with power can make lethal choices for what seem to them at the time the best of reasons, believing that what they're trying to do is in the best interest of an individual and the larger group. Early in my recovery, I was fortunate to embrace abstinence from drugs and to commit myself to people who had a program and a fellowship that supported abstinence. But some years afterward I met resistance from people with power over me. They were unsympathetic to that program and that fellowship, at least in my case. They believed, quite sincerely, that only prolonged treatment, preferably Freudian, and an open-ended regimen of drugs would make me fit to live with.

This frightened me. I believed then, and believe still, that their remedy would kill me. But they made it very clear that I had no other choice. I felt profoundly isolated, since they assured me that all right-thinking, healthy Jesuits felt as they did. But then I remembered a Jesuit I had known fifteen years earlier. We hadn't been friends, largely because he was loaded so much of the time in those days, while I was still pretty tame. An extrovert, he got noisier when he was in his cups, whereas I drank quietly and alone. Indeed, he had been so bad that they wouldn't ordain him unless and until he got sober. So he did, and pioneered recovery for a whole generation of us.

At the height of the campaign to institutionalize me, I wrote him. This was long before email and smartphones, and a conventional long-distance (!) phone call seemed too brash, so I sent him a letter with a stamp on it, as one did in those primordial times. He very quickly sent me a letter with a stamp on it. I opened it. The first line was, "No, Jim, *you* are not crazy."

There was more to the letter, and heaven knows there has been a lot more to our relationship in the more than 30 years since. But even that opening gambit was enough to save my life. I had one independent voice outside a set of relationships shaped by archaic attitudes to alcoholism telling me that I was on the right track.

How has my relationship to this savior evolved since the late 1980s? His corroboration – did you know this word means "sharing strength like an oak tree's"? – gave me the moxie I needed to turn down institutionalization. Instead I proposed to the higher-ups that instead I would simply move to the West Coast and continue my recovery there. Since they were all Midwesterners, they were deeply convinced that everyone on the West Coast was crazy, so they thought this an elegant solution.

Whether or not West Coasters are crazy, I have lived my life out here ever since. It was a fortunate choice. As it happens, Washington, where I live, and California, where my mensch lives, are two states that seem to have responded rather sensibly to the pandemic. In any event, during all the intervening years I have been helpful to the people around me: I spent those thirty years teaching about addictions and being a parish priest. And in my turn I have told other people that they were not crazy, and that they should stick to the recovery that was effective for them.

These days many states are beginning to re-open, but no one is at all sure that this is timely – many predict a worsening of the pandemic, at least in some areas. We are moving very slowly in Washington, and I hope for the sake of hundreds of good friends here that we're choosing the right path. But when it's safe – and no one knows when that will be – I plan to move to California to spend the rest of my days with the man who told me I wasn't crazy.

Chapter 15

Stop Thinking About Tomorrow

One of the most useful remarks I've heard about the pandemic came from an unlikely source – not a doctor or a virus specialist, and not a pundit or a politician, but a very colorful and creative performance artist, Taylor Mac. (Taylor Mac prefers "they, their," for pronouns, and I will honor that preference.) The *New York Times* interviewed several notable people about how they were living through the lockdown. Taylor Mac mostly lives and works in New York City; but for now they were sequestered in upstate New York with their husband. Many people in seclusion say that they have cut themselves off, in whole or in large part, from the news; Taylor Mac was even more specific – they avoid anyone who is trying to guess the future, and focus as much as possible on the present.

ONE MORE TIME: ONE DAY AT A TIME

This seems wise to me, and not just because it's a variant of One Day at a Time. It's also sensible since so many people are trying to predict the post-pandemic world, and there is such a huge difference in the predictions. They range from "We're going to find a cure next week" to "It'll be twelve to eighteen months before a reliable vaccine is generally available," with "We already have a cure – and it's in this bottle available for $29.95!" to "We're never going to find an effective cure" as extremes on either side. Most people seem to think the world of tomorrow will be different, but there is a similar range in how it will be different. Meanwhile, as various states and cities try to reopen, we're told that the rates of infection will 1) go up 2) go down 3) stay the same.

Of course some predictions are more fact-based than others, but for my own mental health I need to regard all of them with detachment. Few of them call for particular action on my part today. I hope that when action becomes more necessary, I will have more and better facts to choose with.

Twelve Step practice does take a look at the past. The middle Steps are about owning our pasts and seeing what we need to do in the present to keep past troubles from recurring. But as one of the Al-Anon daily meditation books puts it, we look at the past, but we don't stare at it. The past has its uses: where else can we find the materials to craft the stories that we tell people to save their lives? Wordsworth famously described poetry as "emotion recollected in tranquility"; the poetry of 12 Step stories could be described as "melodrama recollected in serenity," with a healthy admixture of black comedy.

And of course it's a kindness to ourselves and to others to make reasonable plans for the future. One of the great attractions of alcohol for me was the timelessness of the state that it induces. I would drift off to a place that was "over the rainbow," and in which the mishaps of the past and the fiascos of the future didn't trouble me. Healthy people don't hide from the past or the future. Instead they do what Thoreau suggested: they build castles in the air, but then they put foundations under them. For their foundation, recovering people look to a Higher Power that cares. The *Big Book* uses architectural language to describe the process of coming to believe: "As soon as [someone] can say that [they] believe, or [are] willing to believe, we emphatically assure [them] that [they are] on [their] way. It has been repeatedly proven among us that upon this simple cornerstone a wonderfully effective spiritual structure can be built" (47, from the chapter "We Agnostics").

TOUCH BOTTOM AND RISE

And having a "cornerstone" is invaluable during the seismic shifts of the pandemic. I hear from a lot of people, in recovery or not, that they are losing loved ones these days to overdoses or suicides. These are often adult children or adult grandchildren of friends who have suffered with their loved ones for years and are now losing them in the face of unendurable stress. Even now there is a steep increase in substance abuse, mental illness, and domestic violence – no need for predictions here, it's a daily reality. The death toll from these causes may be every bit as grievous as the losses from the virus.

The wonder is that my recovering friends are talking about their losses in a way that helps them and helps others to stay solidly grounded on their "cornerstone." I try to remind them in conversation, as I'm doing in writing this book, what a great service it is to stay steady when so many people are looking for a place to stand.

Recovering people also perform a great service for those who can't find such a place and give up the struggle. Recovering people remember those who have been lost to the darkness, to drugs, to mental illness. They attend their memorial services, and sometimes are the only people who do.

We can't know what the world after the pandemic will be like, and we can make ourselves crazy trying to guess. But as the song from *Casablanca* puts it, "The fundamental things apply / As time goes by." We can choose today to take with us into the uncertain future the things that matter most – like the readiness to stretch out a hand to those who need it. This belief is enshrined in a Pledge adopted by AA and Al-Anon: I am responsible. When anyone, anywhere, reaches out for help, I want the hand of AA or Al-Anon always to be there. And for that I am responsible.

Recovering people do this; but so do so many doctors and nurses and nursing home workers. Whatever we choose to remember after the pandemic, we "must remember this." In this dark hour, many ordinary women and men laid down their lives by risking illness, or even by working themselves to the point of suicidal exhaustion, in hopes of saving lives.

Medical people take a pledge too, the Hippocratic Oath. It's with that oath that my friend John Whitney, S.J. begins his beautiful memorial to Dr. Lorna Breen, who took her life after saving so many sick people in New York City. The rest of us, with or without a pledge, should focus on service: a principle for the post-pandemic future is that "the particular patient is a human being, fragile and in need, whose very humanity calls out for a response that cannot be ignored" (St. Joseph Parish Bulletin, May 3rd, 2020).

Another Jesuit friend was once in deep doubt about his future. He was struggling with, as they say in so many Covid obituaries, an "underlying condition." On top of that he was having alarming symptoms from another, undiagnosed illness. He was on a retreat at this time, and he found great consolation in a passage from the prophet Jeremiah, who is mostly known for bleak predictions. This passage was different: it was about hope. My friend, a talented composer, made the words into a hymn, part of which goes, "I know the plans I have for you, says the Lord ... to give you a future full of hope." That was many years ago; my friend is still alive, and still composing.

Chapter 16

~❧~

Not All Crazy on the Same Day

The last few days of the pandemic have brought me face to face with the 7th Step, "Humbly asked God to remove our shortcomings." The *12 X 12* talks a lot about humility when it takes up this Step, but oddly enough, humility is defined elsewhere, in the commentary on Step 5: "To those who have made progress in A.A., [humility] amounts to a clear recognition of what and who we really are, followed by a sincere attempt to become what we could be" (58).

This is pretty straightforward, but even so, recovering people often find it difficult to talk about humility, no doubt from fear that if you talk about it, you don't really have it. I get a clearer sense of humility from thinking about its opposite. Actually, alcoholics typically go to the opposite on any given topic.

HUMILITY AND HUBRIS

So what is the opposite of humility? There's a very old concept that fills the bill, I think: it goes all the way back to Aristotle's commentary on Greek tragedy, especially Sophocles' masterpiece *Oedipus the King*.

Aristotle said that tragic heroes like Oedipus suffered from a tragic flaw (*hamartia*, literally a "falling short," like shooting an arrow that doesn't make it all the way to the target). The flaw itself he described as hubris. The word means "pride," but not in the positive sense of self-esteem. It comes from the word for "above" or "over," and it means "too much pride." It's often translated, a little archaically, as "overweening pride."

To return to the *12 X 12*, hubris is a matter of having too great a sense "of what and who we really are." Oedipus thought he was hot stuff because he solved a deadly riddle and became king of Thebes; this led him to launch an investigation into an old crime, which he pursued arrogantly, since he had an inflated sense of his riddle-solving capacity. The irony is that he turns out to be the criminal he's seeking.

This can be put more simply in the words of a modern philosopher who's rather more down to earth than Aristotle. In one of the Dirty Harry movies, Harry Callahan – played with very few facial muscles by Clint Eastwood – says repeatedly, "A man's got to know his limitations." Since Dirty Harry does not suffer from hubris, he doesn't end tragically – the creepy bad guy does. Of course a .357 Magnum helps to make his point.

I have been pondering hubris and humility – the second word is from humus, which means "earth" or "dirt" – at this point in the pandemic because I think I had a hubris slip over the last few days or weeks. As I have said at some points in this book, I had come to think that I was doing pretty well emotionally during the quarantine, in fact rather better than some of those with whom I am locked down. When my superior asked me how I was doing, I put on my best Clint Eastwood and said that I was holding my own, I was Mr. Serenity, thank you very much. Then a few unimportant things happened all at once. My cat seems to have arthritis. Any kind of return to church gatherings where I can use my talent for leading worship is becoming more and more elusive (when? how?). I'm hearing about the mean-spirited treatment of some people I greatly care about: this had happened before the pandemic hit, but I hadn't heard any news of it during the lockdown. Now several people have told me the poor treatment is continuing, and probably won't stop.

MOTHER'S DAY 2020

But what finally put me over the edge was Mother's Day. This year, because of the pandemic, people in the media seemed much more conscious of mothers and adult children than they have in past years. Or maybe I had a lot more time to notice all the stories about mothers and grown daughters and sons on the news. In the middle of one such story, they showed a clip from *Dumbo*: Dumbo's mother has been caged by the Bad People for trying to protect her unusual son, and that night Dumbo finds her there and they twine trunks through the bars, with tears overflowing Dumbo's eyes. It destroyed me.

I'll say more in the next chapter about how much I adored my mother, but what was with me for me the next several days after I revisited Dumbo was that she has now been dead for forty-nine years. Mother's Day this year was also marked for me by two events: it was the fiftieth birthday of my nephew, Matthew, who was born on Mother's Day 1970; and it was the first anniversary of the death from cancer of one of my sponsors, Bob F. So . . . no more Mr. Serenity for me. No more "I'm doing fine, in fact rather better than you poor slobs who don't have a Program." No; I was a mess and told some of my closest recovering friends that I was.

So what else is new. One of my friends quoted the old

saw that the Program works because we're not all crazy on the same day. But on any given day any one of us gets to be the crazy one. That's the humble truth. It's also a saving fact. When I'm crazy, and for as long as I stay that way, I can lean back on the comfort of friends who have had their crazy days too, and will again. I'm no different from, and no better than, anybody else who's trying to get through this pandemic, which is acting on all of us like a chisel on marble. Some days I have no idea how to get to the other side – unless I let go of all the possible, terrifying futures, and deal with what is in front of me today. So I'm not going to pick my cat up and put her on her tower anymore: she used to love being on it, but now it hurts when she eases down from it. Instead I'll join her on the floor, where it doesn't hurt. And tomorrow . . .

Chapter 17

❧

The Top of the Mark

In June 1971 my mother, Rita Brennan Harbaugh, had been in mysteriously failing health for some time. One evening during a family gathering, we were talking about traveling, and the allure of San Francisco came up. She had never been there; suddenly, fiercely, she said, "I want to go to the Top of the Mark!"

This summed up so much about her – her openness and eagerness for new experiences, her desire for a touch of glamor amid interesting people. With only two years of high school, she had worked her way up in early television in St. Louis to the position of writer-producer of a daily talk show. She had booked traveling stars to be on the show and had met them when they came. She was not impressed by a very young Barbra Streisand, but she was

awestruck by the composer Richard Rodgers – I got
enmeshed with Broadway musicals at my mother's knee.
The Top of the Mark is the top floor of the Mark Hopkins
Hotel in the heart of San Francisco, where there was a luxe
piano bar. It was perhaps the most elegant place outside of
Manhattan in the United States. She had done a little
traveling, but my dad was the kind of alcoholic, like me,
who wanted to pass out watching *Green Acres* on the
television at home, so her opportunities for exploring the
world were limited. And two or three weeks after that
family gathering, she died at fifty-six. She never got to the
Top of the Mark.

But her wish came back to me at a crucial juncture of
my life, and I think because of it I've lived – and traveled –
and am still going at seventy-four. I remembered her at a
dramatic moment in my life – and she had a great flair for
drama, which I share. I was in rehab for alcoholism. It was
a twenty-eight-day, Hazelden-model program in Denver. I
had already been a priest for seven years, so I decided
early on in the program that it would be highly
professional of me to assist the counseling staff in helping
the other patients. And sure enough, with my roots in an
alcoholic family, I was darned good at it. I could spot denial
and break down resistance. I could demolish compliance
and nudge toward surrender. Every day I demonstrated
how badly I needed the principals of Al-Anon, but at the
time I just thought I was being helpful.

Finally, near the end of my stay, my counselor, Ros,
decided it was time in small group to work on *me*. She
began the effort by asking me why I thought I deserved to
get and stay sober. This was a poser for me; I couldn't
think of a single reason, largely because I was so ashamed

of being an alcoholic priest. In fact I had become a Jesuit priest mainly because I wanted to leave my lower-class alcoholic roots behind. I had failed.

Ros kept pressing me on why I should be sober. I think we both knew that this was going to be a turning point, but which direction I would turn was still up in the air. First I thought of my dad, his endless pessimism, his gloom, his fatalism about anything good ever coming or staying. That was Option A, since I clearly had his genes.

And then I remembered my mom wanting to go to the Top of the Mark. She was Option B, and the essence of this was life, was risk, was going out into the world and hoping to meet some people I didn't know who would welcome me. Somehow I stammered this out in small group, and the whole group, including Ros, came over and wrapped me in a group hug. I was thinking, "My God, this is *The Snake Pit*, and I'm Olivia de Havilland!" I was deeply embarrassed. But at that moment a door opened, and it's still open now, thirty-seven years later, in the middle of a pandemic with a scary, uncertain future.

No, I never made it to the Top of the Mark. But I've been to Bangkok, and Dublin, and Stockholm. I've been to every one of the fifty states. Amid the pandemic, I'm in touch by Zoom with dear friends who live in Florida, Wisconsin, Minnesota, Texas, and so on.

Last Sunday, Mother's Day, I was as I've said sadder than I am most years on that day. The quarantine, and all the losses people are experiencing now, made my own loss stand out more harshly.

But I also need to remember my mother's strong appetite for life.

The day I said my first Mass as a priest – six years after my mother's death, and seven years before she saved my life during rehab – at the party afterward, one of my sisters asked me how I was feeling. I said, "A song keeps running through my head, 'Everything's Comin' Up Roses!'" Ethel Merman, as Mama Rose, sings it before the first act curtain in *Gypsy*. The part I keep recalling is "You can do it / All you need is a hand / We can do it / Mama is gonna see to it!'" I believed it that day; I believed it in treatment when I had to come up with a reason to live; and now, when I quake at what may come with the pandemic, I believe it still.

Coda

✎✎

Farewell, My Lovely

These 17 chapters are what I had written by mid-May of 2020. As I mentioned earlier, I was taking it a chapter at a time; when I finished Chapter 17, I had some ideas for the next chapter. But then I stopped writing.

This was not because the pandemic was over. Far from it. In the months since, we learned that the pandemic didn't pause during the summer, before gathering strength for Phase II in the fall and winter, as the flu does. On the tragic contrary: just as states and cities across the country were preparing slowly in June to return to normal, there were huge surges in the numbers of the sick and the dying, not just in places that had been incautious about prevention, but also in states like Washington and California, which had adopted strict lock-downs from the beginning. Three months later, in August, there are small and tentative signs that things are improving a little, but that's as far as we've come. If I had wanted to continue to report on living and recovering during the pandemic, by now this book would be twice as long as it is.

No: I stopped in May, when it was just beginning to dawn on us that pandemic life was going to continue unabated, at least on the West Coast. I stopped writing, not because there was nothing more to write about, but because I couldn't continue. Since then I have looked over what I wrote during spring. I have tidied it up a little, but I have left the content unaltered to reflect the fact that we know little more now, in late summer, than we knew then about the future, about the world after the pandemic.

What I can see now in what I wrote, which I didn't see then, are the hints and the warnings about the event that made me stop writing. On May 26 I had to put my cat Leontyne to sleep. Back then I wrote, in Chapter 7, about how close we were, how much we meant to each other. I told you that I rescued her when she was dying on the streets, and then had to – got to – keep her close to me. I didn't mention that when I took her to the vet or sent cellphone pictures of her to friends and family, they all remarked how beautiful she was.

Toward the end of what I wrote then, I began to notice that she was having difficulties climbing and walking. I thought it was age; I thought that, like me, she had arthritis. I took her to her vet, and they agreed, and gave me some medication for her. I was gratefully relieved, and began giving her the medication.

After a day or two, she couldn't move at all. I thought she was reacting to the medication, so I took her, on Friday night of the Memorial Day holiday, to an emergency pet hospital. Again, they agreed with my hunch that it was the medication. They let her sleep it off, and then let me take her home on Saturday evening, but with a warning that she might later need an MRI on her brain if this turned out to be more than an adverse reaction to a powerful pain reliever. We had one more wonderful, normal day on Sunday. And then on Monday she stopped moving again; she couldn't even drink water.

I thought she was having strokes, but since it was a holiday, I waited 24 hours. If this was going to be her last day on earth, I wanted her to be at home, with me. I gave her water from a dropper and stayed by her side. On Tuesday morning, a Jesuit friend who also has a cat drove us to her vet.

The vet was wonderfully kind, even amid the pandemic restrictions. She let me be with Leontyne as she was first given an injection to calm her fears. And then, while I kept stroking her, she was given an infusion. After only a minute or two, the vet gently said, "She's already gone."

Only people who have deeply loved and then lost a pet will know what it's been like for me, at first and in the weeks since. My sister Martha, who lost a cat a year ago, wrote me that "a lady always knows when to leave the room." I wanted three or four more years of Leontyne – we think she was about thirteen this spring – but it's like she was setting me free so I could move to Oakland, California, where I have been since the end of June. I would never have moved if she had just gotten very sick.

Another sign that coming to California then was the right thing: no sooner did I move, with the great help of a much younger Jesuit in my community who was also transferring to the Bay Area, than there was, as I mentioned above, an enormous surge in the numbers of those affected by the virus, in Texas and Florida, but also in California. If we had waited even a few days longer, we might not have been able to move at all.

I have been living now for three months with the old friend I told you about who gave me the courage to move to the West Coast thirty years ago and to continue my recovering journey. Even with the ongoing fear and sadness – and anger – of the pandemic and the poor American response to it, I have known a lot of peace this summer.

The old friend – his name is Tom – has lived with cats for many years. In fact it was he who turned me on to cats in the first place; before I began my new life on the West Coast, I had been a dog person. For a decade he has had two beautiful Burmese cats; the female is rather high-strung, but the male, Nico, has moved in with me. As I write, he's dozing next to Leontyne's cat-tower, which I brought to Oakland with me. I solemnly promised Nico that I would never invidiously compare him to Leontyne, or mourn her in his presence. Tom's niece, Mary, is also supposed to bring us a kitten she has been fostering to add to our Jesuit community in Oakland.

But between us, Nico is sweet but oh no Leontyne. When people meet him, they say, "That's a nice cat," but they don't say "Oh, what a beauty!" He has his graces, but he seems like a California surfer boy next to the depth I saw in her eyes.

We buried her right after she died at the vet's. We interred her in the back yard of the parsonage at St. Leo's, the parish where she and I were so happy in Tacoma. She's not far from the grave of her old boyfriend, Leo the Cat, who first spotted her loveliness. She's on the special pad with her name on it that a parish friend made for her; next to her is her Martha Stewart cat brush.

During her last hours I promised her that I would follow her to wherever she went as soon as I could. Meantime I will take care of myself, especially as a seventy-five-year-old during a pandemic. I will do nothing, actively or passively, to shorten the time until I see her again.

Because that, after all, is What I Learned During the Pandemic. I figured when I began to write that I would pull ideas from the air, a chapter at a time, and only know what it all meant when I had finished writing. I assumed then that the book would end when the pandemic did. Instead, I stopped when I lost the love of my life. But even though the book is shorter than I thought it would be, I know now what I was supposed to learn. It's all about recovery.

There are days when in my grief I wonder if I will ever be of much service to anyone again. All the churches in the Bay Area are supposed to be in lockdown, so I am not needed there. But with the help of Zoom I am more active in 12 Step recovery than I had ever been, in early or later days, before the pandemic hit. Yet even beyond this online service, God's gift of life to me is meant to be reveled in, even if only by me – and Nico.

And now I need to practice these principles one day at a time, as long as the days arrive fresh from the God who loves drunks.

Jim Harbaugh

.

Help for Hard Times

Acknowledgments

Thanks for the existence of this book are due. You would not have it if Annie Lamott had not been faithful all through the writing and editing of it. From her first enthusiasm in June 2020, when I was about to move mid-pandemic from Tacoma to Oakland, through the beautiful forward she wrote in November, to the help her husband, Neal Allen, gave to the final shaping of the book in September 2021, she has been a patient and supportive doula.

Thanks also to Tom Weston, S.J., superior of my Jesuit community in Oakland, who has been an unfailing source of encouragement when the pandemic and other current events got me down, and to the other members of the John Courtney Murray community.

Thanks to my spiritual guides, before and during the pandemic: Dr. Mary Cross, Stephanie Butler, and Fr. Kevin Ballard, S.J., and especially Bob Fuller, who died before the pandemic began but who gave me the push I needed to seek shelter with Tom W.

Jim Harbaugh

Help for Hard Times

Made in the USA
Las Vegas, NV
30 September 2021

31393001R00074